The Little Duchess. The Story of Lord Nelson's Wife.

by

Joyce Gordon

Dedicated to the memory of Ian and to all my family, Madelaine, William, Andrew and my six grandchildren.

Printed and bound in Great Britain by;
Semper Virens Ltd, NorthTawton, Devon

Published by Stanewood Publications.
E-mail: joycegordon@amserve.com

Acknowledgements.

This biography could never have been written without the encouragement of my late husband, Ian Gordon. My family have given me help in many ways. Joan and David Robinson gave me unlimited access to the Museum of Nevis History and Vince Hubbard found interesting material for me in the U.S.A. .Mr and Mrs Edmonson who live in Lady Nelson's former house in Exmouth kindly entertained me there. My late brother, Dr D.W. Cammock helped me with details of Nelson's severed arm. I must also thank Dr Mellisa Hardie of the Hypatia Trust for much encouragement as well as my friend Edwina Vardey. Judith Lowe kindly did the proof reading. Much help and kindness have been shown by the printers. I am indebted to Veronica Kiddersley for the prints from an early edition of Southey's life of Nelson and to Jenny Bidgood for her pictures of Lady Nelson's memorial and her tomb in Littleham Church. My thanks also for the use of portraits supplied by the Royal Naval Museum Portsmouth and the National Maritime Museum Greenwich as well as to The Times Newspapers and Getty Images for the picture of the Little Duchess on the book cover. The staff in South Molton library were very helpful in providing books and information. To all these people and others I am most grateful for their help and encouragement.

CONTENTS

ILLUSTRATIONS

1. Plaque on gate post of Montpelier House, Nevis. Photo by Andrew Gordon

2. Nelson playing with young Josiah Nisbet at Montpelier with John Herbert seen in the background. From an early edition of the Life of Nelson by Robert Southey.

3. Fanny and Nelson portrayed together whilst living at Burnham Rectory, Norfolk. Also from the life of Nelson by Robert Southey

4. Frances Nelson; painted in 1798 . Artist unknown. The National Maritime Museum, Greenwich.

5. Frances Nelson; c1800: attributed to Henry Edridge. This portrait is referred to as 'The waiting wife'. The Royal Naval Museum, Portsmouth.

6. Impression of the memorial to Lady Nelson inside Littleham church Exmouth. Drawing by Jenny Bidgood.

7. The Nisbet tomb in the churchyard at Littleham, photo by Andrew Gordon.

Cover. A portrait of Lady Nelson painted in 1830 by Sir William Beechey. Used by kind permission of Getty Images.

INTRODUCTION

THE EXMOUTH CONNECTION

Inside Littleham Parish Church, Exmouth, on the eastside of the Chantry Chapel there is a Memorial to Lady Nelson. Cast in Italian marble, a woman is depicted lying prostrate over a tomb. Underneath are inscribed the words

"Sacred to the memory of FRANCES HERBERT NELSON DUCHESS OF BRONTE widow of the late Admiral Lord Viscount Nelson and to her son Josiah Nisbet Esq ,Captain in the Royal Navy whom she survived eleven months and died in London May 6th 1831 aged 73 years.
This humble offering of affection is erected by Frances Herbert Nisbet in grateful remembrance of those virtues which adorned a kind mother-in-law and a good husband."

In the churchyard is a sarcophagus made of grey Portland stone surrounded with railings which contains the bodies of Lady Nelson, her son and his four children.

Horatio Nelson became England's greatest naval hero, his fame enshrined by the nation. His statue stands at the top of the towering column in London's Trafalgar Square. Many books describe his career and exploits; there are Nelson Museums, Nelson chronicles, Nelson Societies and thousands of people visit his birthplace annually. Frances Nelson had no claim to such fame, her only purpose in life being that of a loving wife and mother. At the time of her death in 1831 she received scant recognition. Most of her husband's biographers have dismissed her as neurotic and dull, incapable of understanding her husband's achievements or the value of his services to the country. She knew fame and neglect, she experienced much grief and sadness, always remaining loyal to Nelson. She is still revered on the Island of Nevis, where she was born. Her tomb has recently been restored by the 1805 Club in association with the Exmouth Society and the Nisbet Society.

My interest in Lady Nelson began when I went to live on Nevis in 1981. In the Nelson Museum I found items of interest relating to both Horatio and Fanny Nelson, yet so little is known about the latter. Far more is known and written about Emma, Lady Hamilton, who supplanted Fanny in Nelson's affections. Emma has featured in a plethora of books, novels, a film, and her portraits by George Romney are familiar to many. Fanny, to the contrary, never sought public attention or notoriety but she does deserve to be known about and understood. This is the story of Lady Nelson, written in the hope that as the bicentenary of Trafalgar approaches, readers will know that Nelson had a loving wife as well as a flamboyant mistress amongst the women of his life.

CHAPTER ONE

THE SUGAR ISLAND

Frances Nelson, formerly Nisbet, neé Woolward, was born in 1761 on the Island of Nevis in the West Indies. Nevis had been described as the proudest island on the Caribees, a place inexpressibly beautiful. A century earlier it was considered the most promising place to make a fortune. It became a British Colony in 1628. Tobacco was the first crop to be grown until sugar became more profitable. Everything connected with sugar dominated the island's history for two centuries.

The island attracted settlers from every walk of life. Royalists such as the Herberts, the Stapletons and the Russells came out from England during the Commonwealth period. Azariah Pinney was deported to the island, having taken part in the Monmouth Rebellion. Others came out seeking cheaper land and prospects than were to be found in England or Scotland. A Jewish community, all of whom were merchants during the late 17th and early 18th centuries settled there.

The plantation owners, the plantocracy, strove to make sufficient wealth from cultivation of sugar for them to return to their mother country and then to live there in comfort and style. The production of sugar depended entirely on slave labour brought from Africa. The slaves worked in the cane fields, the sugar mills and the sugar factories, some also working as domestic servants. At the time of Fanny's birth there were 10,000 slaves on Nevis, a proportion of ten black to one white person. There was a safe market for sugar in England, consumption had risen seven and a half times during the 18th century.

This white Creole society had narrow interests and little in the way of culture. Their every day lives were dull though eminent visitors were subjected to feasting and parties, giving the impression of elegance and ostentatiousness. The Anglican Church was poorly supported and their political enthusiasm was also lukewarm. Drinking was a major diversion along with cock fighting, during which ladies were served tea. The women had little to occupy their lives. Most of them married before the age of twenty, many of the marriages between planter families.

Clothing was ordered frequently from London, Antigua being the nearest place to buy certain basic items. Few of the women took any interest in the running of the estates. They had adequate help to run their houses and look after their children so they spent their time visiting one another, being driven in carriages using the Upper Round road to reach certain of the plantations. Sons were sent to school in England, whereas daughters usually remained on the island sharing tutors and being taught essential subjects. These included French, music, painting and embroidery, with some attention to manners and eloquence.

Fanny spent all her childhood years on Nevis. Her mother had died when she was barely two years old. The maternal line, the Herberts, were descended from the Earls of Pembroke and had come to the Island two generations earlier. (Fanny always kept the letter H in her signature for this reason.) She knew little about her father's family except that his father had been a Mariner. Not a planter himself, her father was Clerk to the Court, then later became the senior

9

Judge and elected to the Island's Assembly. She was an only child, and spent most of her time with her cousins, Martha Herbert, Sally and Magnus Morton. Her own home was small compared to some of the Great Houses built on the plantations, Mr Woolward employed servants for both indoor and outside duties. Fanny was looked after by Cato who attended to her every need and whom she loved dearly. She shared teachers with her cousins for classes in basic scholastic subjects. Little time was spent out of doors; the Creole society were fearful of the harm done to their skins by the rays of the sun.

Her uncle John Herbert owned a large plantation, Montpelier. He was one of the first to have a windmill built instead of a cattle mill. It was said that his stock of Negroes was worth £600 and in good years he would send 500 casks of sugar to Bristol. Sugar was grown all over the island apart from the highest slopes of Mount Nevis which was covered with trees. Fanny would have seen the slaves at work, planting, hoeing and finally cutting the sugar cane which was then loaded onto wagons, pulled by oxen and taken to the sugar mills. The pungent smell of the boilings used to pervade the island during harvest time. Driving around the island there was always a view of the sea, with ships sailing close to the coast or coming into the port at Charlestown. The neighbouring islands of St Kitts could be seen from the western and northern shores and Montserat from the eastern side.

Many grim events took place in the decade of the 1770s. In August 1772 a severe hurricane occurred. Fanny was then twelve years old. Every family stayed in their homes with shutters and doors bolted, listening to the terrifying noise of the wind and torrential rain, only emerging when the force of the wind had lessened to witness devastation beyond belief. Trees uprooted, buildings damaged, water gushing down the ghauts, roads awash and the sugar crop ruined. Many slaves died of starvation that year.

The outbreak of the American War in 1775 brought great hardship The planters were in sympathy with the American Colonists, as they also objected to the trade restrictions and taxes which were imposed on them from Britain. When France joined the war on the side of the Americans, food and supplies became difficult to import and very costly. The island's defences had to be improved, the forts and the batteries were manned day and night. The island was in constant fear of invasion, there having been a previous invasion by the French in 1706 when the damage done to the island had been catastrophic and the British government voted a sum of £100,000 to recompense the planters.

In 1779 Fanny's entire life changed. Her father sustained an injury and developed lockjaw. Despite the efforts of Dr Josiah Nisbet he suffered pain and agony, Fanny watching him die. They had been close to each other since her mother's death. At his funeral he was shown great respect by his many friends and the island's officials, having served on the Assembly for six years. He was buried beside his wife in the churchyard at St John's Church. Some time later Fanny had a memorial erected to both of them mounted on the wall inside the church. There was very little money for Fanny to inherit, her father's share in the firm Herbert, Morton and Woolard was negligible. Their house was sold as were the servants except for Cato, whose freedom had been bought by John Herbert and she remained with Fanny. John Herbert invited Fanny to live with his family at Montpelier, an invitation she gladly accepted.

CHAPTER TWO

MRS Josiah NISBET

Dr Josiah Nisbet made frequent calls at Montpelier in the course of his duties attendant on the health of the slaves employed on the estate. On each occasion he also called at the house to see Fanny, enquiring after her health and showing great concern towards her. A warm relationship soon developed between them, which was more than a platonic friendship. Josiah was twelve years older than Fanny and had known her since she was a child. His family owned Mount Pleasant, a plantation set high on the northern slopes of Mount Nevis. His father had come from Ayrshire in Scotland and he had married Miss Webb from New River Estate.

Four children had been born before his mother had died in 1752. Josiah, being the second son, and knowing he was unlikely to inherit the estate, had decided to study medicine in Edinburgh, where he qualified as a doctor. Upon his return to Nevis he was employed to tend the health of the slaves on several of the largest plantations, as well as being consulted by planters and their families. Mr Pinney at Montravers had a hospital for his slaves in a disused boiler house, and at Old Manor there was a birthing room to ensure that the women slaves who gave birth had a better chance of survival. Dr Nisbet was regarded as a man of sensibilities, more intellectual than most of the other male members of the plantocracy. He did not make much of a fortune from his profession. Payment was frequently made to him in kind, sugar or rum, or on an annual basis that all too often did not materialise.

To Fanny he was the brother she had never had; his interest and affection for her replaced the love her father had shown her. She loved him dearly and trusted him in every way. Before their engagement was announced Josiah had told Fanny of his intention of leaving Nevis to return to England to find work near his uncle who lived close to Salisbury. There were several reasons for this, financial being one, another his health. Having been infected with and survived Yellow Fever he needed to live in a cooler climate. Thirdly, Josiah like others on the island, was aware that profits from sugar were diminishing and that the long-term prosperity of the island was bleak.

The marriage between Josiah and Fanny took place at Montpelier in June 1779. John Herbert gave Fanny away and the Nisbet family, the Herberts and close friends all celebrated and wished them happiness before they set sail for England.

They sailed to Bristol in one of Mr Pinney's sugar boats, the fare paid was £6 each. It was a hazardous journey knowing that they might well encounter the French with whom England was still at war. After six weeks Fanny had her first sight of England when they docked at Bristol. The size of the town, the busy streets, the throngs of people everywhere were new experiences for her. After staying with friends in Bristol (where there were several Nevis connections) they took the coach to Salisbury. Riding in coaches and lodging at inns on the way were also new experiences for her as was the sight of the English countryside, the rolling hills and picturesque villages, the muddy roads and the leafless trees, it being winter time. Josiah's uncle George Webb welcomed them into his home at Stratford-sub-Castle, a village close to Salisbury.

A house in the Cathedral town was found to rent and a servant engaged. Life in Salisbury was very different from life on Nevis. Perhaps they attended services in the Cathedral, perhaps Fanny enjoyed seeing the hustle and bustle which took place on market days when stalls were set up and carts came in from the countryside laden with produce.

It was hoped that the temperate climate would help Josiah to gather strength, but he continued to suffer from bronchial problems and became wan in his appearance.

Fanny gave birth to their son in 1780; he was named Josiah and christened in the church at Stratford-sub-castle. During the following year Dr Nisbet's health deteriorated and there was no way of preventing his steady decline until he died.

Fanny was prostrate with grief. George Webb acted for her, arranging the funeral and burial which took place in the church at Stratford-sub Castle. High on the wall of the sanctuary there is a tablet which reads "Josiah Nisbet. M.D. of the island of Nevis, born 1747 died 5 October 1781. This monument was erected by his affectionate wife Frances Nisbt" Above the tablet is the Nisbet coat of arms and close by is a tablet in memory to Josiah's cousin, Joseph Webb who died "of a decline in the first day of the year 1779 at the premature age of 25"

There was no inheritance for Fanny, no money had been made for Josiah's medical work and his inheritance from his family was involved in the Mount Pleasant plantation which his elder brother Walter now owned. She was shown sympathy and comfort and generosity by the Webbs and friends in Bristol. As soon as the news of her bereavement reached Nevis, John Herbert sent word to Fanny to return there to live with his family. He wanted Fanny to run his household. There had been an unfortunate disagreement between him and his daughter Martha concerning her wish to marry Mr Hamilton, whom her father considered unsuitable. Martha did not excel in any domestic pursuits nor did she show interest in her social obligations. Fanny knew she would not be offending her cousin if she returned to Nevis as suggested.

It was two years before Fanny and her son, young Josiah, could return to Nevis. During those two years Nevis had been occupied by the French. On 9th January 1782 a fleet of 24 sail-of-the line under Admiral Francios de Grasse had been seen sailing directly to Nevis. John Herbert and the Council decided to capitulate, their defences were inadequate and their militia numbered less than 300. John Pinney and James Tobin negotiated terms with the French Land Commander and the island was then disarmed and treated as neutral. 5,000 troops were stationed on St Kitts, where the British on Brimstone Hill were besieged for thirty five days before surrendering and being forced to capitulate. During the occupation of Nevis conditions were not easy, the French Officers were civil and polite to the planters but the greatest problem was providing enough food for the entire population as only neutral ships could officially bring in supplies. The island was restored to Britain following the Peace of Versailles in 1783.

Mr and Mrs John Pinney, influential friends of Fanny's who owned several plantations on Nevis as well as sugar boats, arrived back in Bristol in 1783, having left the West Indies for good. It was these friends who made all the arrangements for Fanny and her young son to return sailing aboard one of his boats, the Edward. There were few passengers but a heavy cargo of dried foods and hardware which had been in short supply during the French occupation. Fanny must have been overjoyed to see Nevis on the horizon with its cloud covered peak, and then to be welcomed home by her relations and friends.

CHAPTER THREE

THE SECOND WEDDING ON NEVIS

"I, William Jones, Clerk, Rector of the parishes of St John and St Thomas in the said island do hereby certify that Horatio Nelson esq. Captain of His Majesty's Ship the Boreas and Frances Herbert Nisbet widow, were married this eleventh day of March in the year of our Lord 1787 according to the canons and constitutions of the church of England at the dwelling house of the Honourable John Richardson Herbert (President of His Majesty's Council and deputy ordinary of the said island) in the aforesaid parish of St John. Given under my hand the day and year above written. Will Jones."

Fanny had been living at Montpelier for two years before she met Horatio Nelson. Her uncle treated her as a second daughter and Josiah as his grandson. Martha and a spinster sister of John Herbert's, Sarah, were the other members of the family. Receiving callers and welcoming visitors were part of Fanny's duties, as well as organising the household. She was regarded as one of the few diligent housekeepers on the island and was very popular among the various families.

There was only one town on the island, Charlestown, where Fanny was able to buy items of food and essentials. It was not an attractive place, being only one street with a few stores. On the sea front stood warehouses and store rooms close to the pier. The residents of the town were merchants, officials and tradesmen. It was possible to buy some things such as corn, flour, dried peas, salt pork, candles, soaps and dried meats but stocks frequently ran out. Many items had to be ordered direct from England, especially wines. Fanny rarely entered a shop or store but would call at the door to make an order or choose what she needed.

Importing sufficient food for the island's population was still a difficulty as only meat, fish and vegetables were to be found locally. Neutral ships brought in supplies but never enough. The British Navy had temporarily lost control of the sea. The North American colonies had become the United States of America, and therefore no longer part of the British Empire. Only limited trade was allowed with the American States and certain items of export or import could only be carried in British ships. Prices soared and the difficulties of everyday life continued.

It was at this time that Horatio Nelson was given command of the 24-gun Frigate, H.M.S. Boreas, stationed in English Harbour on Antigua, arriving in July 1784. He took shelter there during the next two months when hurricanes could occur. He then sailed around the Leeward Isles examining anchorages and facilities for water for the ships. Nelson observed that the authorities on every island were trading with American vessels, thereby flouting the Navigation Laws and offending his own strong personal sense of duty. The first time he sailed into Charlestown on Nevis he observed four heavily laden American ships about to unload their cargo. He ordered them to leave within forty-eight hours. They refused to comply and Nelson seized the ships and cargoes. Such dramatic action was totally alien to the planters, who were irate at the loss of the supplies and the trade. The Captains of the ships proceeded to claim damages from Nelson amounting to £40,000. To avoid arrest Nelson remained concealed aboard for several days. Despite the fact that Mr Herbert was effected by Nelson's strict policy he offered to put up bail of £10,000 for his release. The case came before the prosecuting lawyer and Nelson himself pleaded the case so well that the goods carried by the offending ships were condemned.

A cousin of Fanny's had written comments regarding Horatio, who was visiting St Kitts. *"We have at last seen the little Captain of the Boreas of whom so much has been said. He was very silent... he declined drinking any wine until the President had given the usual toast. There was a sternness in his behaviour as well as a reserve which made conversation a strain..if you Fanny had been there we think you could have made something of him, you have a habit of attending to these odd sort of people."* The little Captain was not considered to be particularly handsome, barely 5'4" tall, he rarely dressed well, his hair was often untidy and bedraggled.

John Herbert gave Horatio an open invitation to call at Montpelier, which he gladly accepted whenever his duties brought him to Nevis. He had been several times before he met Fanny. On one occasion he had been found playing on the floor with Josiah when Mr Herbert entered the room. Fanny and Horatio met at a Montpelier dinner party when Fanny thanked him for being so friendly to her son, now aged five. They soon were on amicable terms with each other and were frequently seen in each others company. The crew of Boreas collected water from the village of Cottonground and whilst this was happening Horatio would climb up Saddle Hill which was close to Montpelier. A battery had recently been constructed there from where he could scan the horizon in search of enemy ships. He regarded Nevis as one of the most beautiful islands in the Caribbean. He was accepted socially and was entertained by various notable families. John Jefferies one of the Nevis grandees who owned Valley estates asked Horatio to be God father to his son George. Fanny and Horatio attended balls at the Bath Hotel. This was the largest hotel in the West Indies, guests came from far afield to enjoy its facilities as well as partaking in its medical baths. They could wander through the gardens and from the roof top, gaze at the stars and the view of St Kitts.

Prince William had come to serve in the Leeward Isles in 1786 as Captain of the Pegasus. He and Horatio had first met four years previously, and mutually respected each other, his presence in the Caribbean meant that Horatio had to accompany him on official occasions as his aide de camp. The Prince had a reputation for being flirtatious and volatile, often dancing until the early hours of the morning. On the occasion of Prince William's first visit to the island £800 was spent for a celebration. One hundred men sat down to dinner with him and seventy ladies were at the ball, including Fanny who had the honour of dancing with the Prince. Horatio's duties accompanying his Royal Highness often left him in a state of fatigue, three days dancing also knocked up some of the fair sex. He loved to honour the Prince although he did not consider it was his province to attend on great men.

When Horatio proposed to Fanny she duly accepted. She had learnt a lot about him, that his father was a Clergyman of very slender means, that his mother who had been part of the Walpole family had died when he was nine years old. He had told her about his brothers and sisters and how he had decided to join the Navy having been encouraged by his mother's brother, William Suckling. She knew that his ambition was to prosper in the Navy but that so far he had had 'no luck'. She knew he was not wealthy but that he was ambitious and did not lack self assurance. She had a great affection for him, but did not show any unrestrained passion. She felt that Horatio would be an affectionate father for Josiah, and she did not want to 'wear the spinster's cap'.

In the first letter which Horatio wrote to Fanny, dated 19 August 1785 he addressed her as "Dear Mrs Nisbet" then "My dear Fanny" and later "My dearest Fanny" a term he used until their separation. He expressed his love for her in his letter *"Most dearly do I love you and trust your affection is not only founded upon the principle of reason but also upon the basis of mutual attachment. My age is enough to make me seriously reflect upon what I have offered and common sense tells me what a good choice I have made."* Later he wrote *"Daily I thank God who ordained that I should be attached to you. He has, I firmly believe intended it as a blessing to me and I am convinced that you will not disappoint His beneficient intentions. Fortune, that is money, is the only thing I regret the want of for the sake of my affectionate Fanny"* He ended his letters 'ever your most affectionate Horatio Nelson' often sending his love to Josiah. When he related gossip from Barbados or St Kitts or Antigua he used a code based on the first letters of people's names. When he was told there had been an outbreak of smallpox and that a number of people had been nursed in Monpelier he replied that it would be a fine place to be sick in but should not be used as an infirmary. He showed a domestic side to his nature by offering to purchase items for Fanny and the Herbert household that could not be bought on Nevis and often sent over his collection of newspapers. On Fanny's behalf he visited Mr Burke on Antigua who was her lawyer and who was settling her affairs connected with the late Dr Nisbet's estate. Horatio's health and his battle with the mosquitoes were all items of news. He hated English Harbour on Antigua and called it a hell hole.

John Herbert had given his approval to the engagement by November 1785,after some hesitancy. On 14 November Horatio wrote to his uncle, William Suckling, Collector of Customs in London, asking him for financial assistance.. *"you will smile and say this Horatio is in love. My present attachment is of pretty long standing but I was determined to be fixed before I broke this matter to any person The lady is Mrs Nisbet, widow of a Dr Nisbet who died 18 months after her marriage and left her with an infant son. From her infancy..... she has been brought up by her mother's brother, Mr Herbert President of Nevis ... her age is 22 and her personal accomplishments you will I suppose I think equal to any person I ever saw, but without vanity her mental accomplishments are superior to most people of either sex and we shall come together as two persons most sincerely attached to each other from friendship. Her son is under her guardianship but totally independent of her .... Herbert is very rich and proud. He has only one daughter and this his niece who he looks upon in the same light if not higher. I have lived in his house since June last and am a great favourite of his. I have told him I am as poor as Job but he tells me he likes me and I am descended from a good family which his pride likes. But he also says' Nelson I am proud and I must live myself therefore I can't do much in my lifetime but when I die she shall have twenty thousand pounds and if my daughter dies before me she shall posses the major part of my property. I intend going to England in 1787 and shall remain there for my life, therefore if you two can live happily together till that event takes place you have my consent ...* " The letter continues, asking his uncle to help him... *"to do something, my future happiness I give my honour is now in your power" he offers to return any sum when he can afford it. "I think Herbert will be brought to give her two or three hundred during his life and if you give me ... either one hundred a year for a few years or a thousand pounds, how happy you will make a couple who will pray for you for ever ... Pray let me know your generous action by the first packet".* The reply from his uncle implied that help would be available if necessary

The date of the wedding was finally decided to fit in with the itinerary of Prince William, who had not only expressed a wish to attend the wedding but to give Fanny away in marriage. Mr Herbert, having hesitated to give his consent to the marriage provided a truly grand spectacle. He no longer fretted

21

that the 'little Captain' would not be able to keep his much loved niece and her son in comfort, though perhaps not the style she had enjoyed with him. Everyone in the household took part in the preparations. A special dinner service of Royal Worcester china was shipped out from England. It was to be the last and biggest social gathering at Montpelier as he had decided to retire to England.

The guests who attended the wedding included planters and their families as well as some of the naval personnel serving on Boreas and Pegasus. They walked around the gardens, feasting, drinking and taking shade under the cotton silk trees. Fanny was dressed in a frock made from Limerick lace with Josiah as her attendant. The two Naval Captains were attired in full dress uniform of blue and white and gold, a splendid sight. Prince William made a speech ending with a toast to the 'principal favourite of the island'.

Their honeymoon was brief, Horatio being ordered to return to England sailing on 17th June. He wanted Fanny and Josiah to sail home with him on the Boreas but Fanny felt she must remain to attend the wedding of her cousin Martha to Mr Andrew Hamilton, since finally her uncle had given his consent to this marriage. The Herberts, Fanny and Josiah sailed back to England on a sugar boat, the Roehampton, arriving in England several weeks after Horatio.

In a letter from Prince William to Lord Hood dated 15th March 1787 he wrote…

"From thence we all proceeded to Nevis..Here we remained a week. Nelson introduced me to his bride, she is a pretty and sensible woman and may have a good deal of money if her uncle Mr Herbert thinks proper. Poor Nelson is head over ears in love. I frequently laugh at him about it. However, seriously my Lord he is more in need of a nurse than a wife. I do not think he can live long..he married Mrs Nisbet on the 11th of March, and I had the honour of

giving her away. He is now for it. I wish him well and happy and that he may not repent the step he has taken."

Another comrade of Nelson's, Captain Thomas Pringle, had a different view of the marriage. He told a mutual friend,

"The Navy, Sir, yesterday lost one of its greatest ornaments by Nelson's marriage. It is a national loss that such an officer should marry; had it not been for that occasion I foresaw that Nelson would become the greatest man in the service."

Nelson's marriage was a surprise and unpredicted by his family and friends despite their two year engagement. Horatio found Fanny physically attractive, pretty with delicate features, dark grey eyes and light brown hair and she had a considerable social position on Nevis. The island provided a background conducive for any romance. Nelson had only recently parted from Mary Moutray, the married lady by whom he had been captivated when he arrived at Antigua. She and her husband had befriended him and made his life there bearable until her husband was recalled to England on account of his ill health. On Nevis he found a similar lady but one who was available. During those years of courtship, much of it in their letters, his admiration, his respect and his longing for Fanny had deepened.

Nelson's upbringing in the parsonage probably influenced his sexuality. The whores and the prostitutes who were sought after by his fellow officers were not to his liking (though he did have a certain 'Dolly' in Leghorn at a later date, and after his marriage). He looked for women he could idolize and respect, someone to replace the mother he had loved but hardly known. So when Captain Nelson accepted the invitation to visit President Herbert at Montpelier,

23

it was at a time when he badly needed someone to love, someone to respect him and to attend to his many needs. For the moment and some time to come, that someone was Frances Nisbet.

CHAPTER FOUR

CAPTAIN AND MRS NELSON IN NORFOLK

Life was not easy for the Nelsons when they arrived in England. The Boreas was detailed to the humiliating task of 'receiving', lying off the Nore at the mouth of the Thames. Nelson's hopes of getting command of another ship did not materialise and he was deeply offended by the treatment he received from the Admiralty. He had expected recognition and appreciation for his services in the Leeward Isles, little realising how unpopular his zealous enforcement of the Navigation Acts had made him. He threatened to resign until he was dissuaded by Lord Hood and placated by his wife. Lodgings were taken for Fanny and Josiah in Great Marlborough Street, where Horatio joined them when not on duty. The Herberts rented a house in Cavendish Square, then on the outskirts of London. The Nelsons joined them there for Christmas celebrations.

Fanny suffered from the fog and the smoke, which covered the London area. When it was not foggy it was raining and the sun never seemed to shine. Any plans they might have had for living in London were abandoned. Horatio showed little sympathy for Fanny's indispositions, which seemed unjust to her considering how she had understood when he had suffered from the heat and mosquitoes in Antigua.

After Christmas Nelson was 'paid off' and put on half pay. The family of three embarked on a tour, firstly going to Bath, Bristol and as far as Exmouth, visiting Fanny's cousin, Sally Kelly. Travelling by coach they continued on their way meeting all the members of the Nelson family. A brother, Maurice, lived near London. Horatio had helped him out of his financial difficulties at one time. Maurice worked as a clerk in the Navy Office and was Horatio's favourite brother.

From there they went to Norfolk to stay with William, the eldest brother. He was Rector of Hillborough, having recently taken Holy Orders. Although these two brothers were close in age they were very different in character, William had originally joined the Navy but had abandoned it. He was pompous and was always referred to as the Rector. Whilst they were there it was decided that Josiah should attend the nearby Grammar School, staying with William, his wife Sarah and their family during the term time. It seemed the best solution to his schooling. Fanny was thankful that at least he would come to her during the school holidays, unlike friends on Nevis whose sons went off to be educated in England for years at a time and were barely recognisable by their parents on reunion.

Their next visit was to the Matchams, George and Kitty, the latter being Horatio's eldest sister. They lived in fine style in a grand house near the Norfolk Coast. Fanny considered George the most unsettled man she had ever met because he moved houses so frequently. He was charming, handsome and cultured as well as being wealthy, having made money in the East Indies. Susannah Bolton, the youngest sister, and her husband Thomas lived near Norwich, and were not as well off as the Matchams. Susannah had been a shop assistant in a village shop near her home until she married her farmer husband.

It was November 1788 before Fanny met her father-in-law, the Reverend Edmund Nelson. Horatio was intending to go to France to improve his knowledge of French and to try to understand the French people, but on being

26

rejoined with his favourite son, his father's joy was so great, giving him new life, that the plan to visit France was quickly abandoned. Horatio was assured by his father that some Norfolk air would do him good. His own infirmities were increasing and he had aged much since last seeing Horatio.

The Rectory was a rambling L shaped house, three storeys high, the downstairs rooms were stone flagged which made the whole house feel cold. The view northwards looked towards the marshes and the surrounding garden had been neglected as much as the interior of the house for Mrs Nelson had been dead for twenty years. Two servants were employed but the housekeeping had to be kept tight as Horatio received only £200 yearly.

The years at Burnham were seldom happy for either Fanny or Horatio. Fanny hated the long winters when cold winds blew in from Russia across the North Sea. The countryside was bleak and featureless, no mountains, few trees. There were mists and frost for weeks on end, roads became impassable. Fanny often took to her bed wrapped in a large moreen. The happiest times were when Josiah returned for his school holidays. They had only a few acquaintances in the neighbourhood and were regarded as the poor relations of distant cousins, the Walpoles at Wolverton Hall. It was humiliating for Horatio to collect his pay from Mr Coke at Holkam Hall; he would have liked to have been better acquainted with him but was treated as a servant.

Early in the new year 1789, Suckling Nelson, the youngest son, returned home. He had tried to trade in groceries in the local town, but having made no success at this his Father was arranging for him to enter Cambridge University to study divinity. Then another of Horatio's brothers, Edmund, came home. He was very ill,dying. Sadness prevailed over the whole family, Horatio organised Edmund's funeral paying extraordinary attention to detail, an example of his exactness and orderliness in everything he did.

27

Horatio had more to occupy him than Fanny did (Only occasionally did she feel inclined to do some painting). He used to ride his pony over to the seaport of Overy Stathes to watch the activities there, the fishing boats and the boat building. It was an escape for him to be alone with his own thoughts to wander along the beach or to read a newspaper undisturbed. He took over farming the Glebe, 30 acres of land adjoining the Rectory on which he grew vegetables for the household and some corn. Sometimes they would go for walks in the woods, listening and looking for birds, Horatio reviving the memories of his childhood. When Josiah was at home he would accompany Horatio much of the time and was encouraged to have an interest in all things connected with the sea.

When Horatio was not busy with practical pursuits he was writing letters to the First Lord of the Admiralty requesting employment and stating that although peace had been declared, the French were busy making renewed efforts to strengthen their positions on land and at sea. The replies he received discouraged and depressed him. He became irritable and at times furious. He kept in touch with Prince William, asking him for employment and even suggesting that Fanny might be a Lady-in-Waiting at Court. Such an offer was not taken up.

Horatio was away from home on the day when two men came to serve a Writ on him for £100,000, relating to trading losses abroad incurred by companies whom he had reported for transgressing international agreements. Fanny received these officials, but was totally bewildered and frightened. When Horatio heard the news he threatened to go abroad immediately unless the Treasury came to his aid. They did promptly.

The months and years passed slowly and tediously. Fanny became adept at being economical and prudent, managing on a meagre income. The ardour and

28

tenderness between them had faded and the marriage remained childless, though Horatio regarded Josiah as his own. Their father, after wintering in Bath in 1789 moved into a rented cottage at Burnham Ulph, thinking perhaps he was intruding upon their privacy. Possibly there had been post-natal complications following Josiah's birth unknown to them. Did they practise 'chastity' by choice or did the circumstances in which they were trapped cause them to be sexually inactive? None of this is known or commented upon.

It was not until early in 1792 that the news from France indicated that war would be inevitable. The whole country was in a state of alertness against the radical ideas spreading across the Channel. Revolution in France seemed imminent following the 'September massacres' there. After Christmas spent with his family Horatio took the coach to London and presented himself at the Admiralty. He was warmly greeted by the First Lord and Lord Hood.

Captain Nelson was ordered to commission the Agamemnon, 64-guns. He returned to Norfolk jubilant, delighted with the prospect before him. He then proceeded to recruit volunteers to serve with him. He was joined by sons of neighbours and other clergymen's sons, before he went to find men from Newcastle, Whitby and Yarmouth. Before his departure he gave a farewell party at the local inn, The Plough, for all his family and friends. He never forgot Burnham Thorpe and would have been buried there if he had been less famous.

Josiah's future career and prospects had been discussed by his parents. There was no possibility of him inheriting money to take up any profession, so the decision was taken for him to serve under Nelson, as a midshipman. He was now aged 12, the same age that Horatio had been when joining the Navy. His mother tended to be tearful rather than enthusiastic about the decision, at the thought of both husband and son leaving her to fight a war against the French.

She was kept busy 'fitting out' her son and buying necessary clothing and equipment for Horatio until their departure. Once aboard the Agamemnon Horatio wrote that "Josiah and myself came down very comfortably yesterday morning, he seems to be very settled and now at home.' For Horatio 'the sunshine has come after the storm".

The ship set sail in May heading for the Mediterranean. From Chatham he wrote reprimanding Fanny for not sending all the things he required on board. This was always a failing of hers and a complaint of his. She assumed that in all matters to do with his life on board ship that he was best left to organise his own affairs. He also told her how delighted he was to be in command of a ship once again. This was something that Fanny never really accepted. She was always fearful for him, which he could not appreciate or understand. She did not realise that being at sea brought out every fine aspect of his character, parts that she never knew existed.

CHAPTER FIVE

AND SO TO BATH

Four years passed before the Nelsons were reunited. When they were, Fanny welcomed into her arms a husband who had lost the sight of one eye and an arm, and whose hair was whitened. He had aged far beyond his years. During that time Nelson had been kept on active service with the Mediterranean Fleet. Toulon, Tunis, Corsica and Cadiz were all places where he had excelled himself. In 1796 he was promoted to Commodore and given command of the 74-gun battleship Captain. He was promoted to Rear Admiral following the Battle of St Vincent in 1797 and made a Knight of the Bath, taking command of the Theseus in the same year. It was during the blockade of Cadiz that he suffered the loss of his right arm and came very close to losing his life, if he had not been helped by Josiah.

The first letters that Fanny wrote to Horatio took over a month to reach him. She was then instructed to send them in the care of HM Consul at Leghorn. Even then it took between three and six weeks for her weekly letters to arrive. His from Corsica had to be fumigated and were difficult to decipher.

Always his letters opened 'My dearest Fanny' and ended 'believe me to be your most affectionate husband Horatio Nelson.' Many of Fanny's letters included 'Love to Josiah' and she even sent instructions for Josiah to be told to clean his teeth 'not crossways but upwards and downwards'. Horatio kept Fanny informed about Josiah from the first day he was at sea, when he felt seasick. In many letters 'Josiah is well and a good boy but as I have often told you not very fond of writing letters'.

31

The boy and his friends from Norfolk, William Hoste, John Weatherhead and William Bolton, were all treated as family by Nelson. They were subjected to a strict discipline, mixing with adult men and looking forward to the prospects of some prize money. In December Josiah wrote,

"Dear Mother - I have been very well since I wrote to you last and hope you have been so. I hope Mr Nelson is very well. I still like being at sea and hope I always shall. We have been at Toulon which I think a very strong place. The Spaniards have run away every time they have engaged the French and have behaved with the utmost barbarity to all those who laid down their arms and also the Neapolitans who behaved very cruelly in some cases. Josiah Nisbet"

It would have been unbearable for Fanny to remain at Burnham alone for such long periods, so instead she spent twelve months on a round of visits to her relations and friends. Very few of the letters she wrote to Horatio during this time have been preserved. Possibly the missing ones were those destroyed by Horatio prior to the naval attack on Santa Cruz.

Her first visit was to Uncle Suckling, who lived in Kentish Town, then a long stay with the Matchams who have moved to Ringwood in Hampshire, then to Norfolk where she stayed first with the Rector and family at Hillborough, then to the Walpoles at Wolverton and at Aylsham. Afterwards, Fanny went to Bath where she met old friends from Nevis, such as Mrs Webb and Mrs Tobin, stayed with the Pinneys in Bristol, and also met her Nisbet relations, Mr and Mrs Lockhart, who lived near Glasgow and Miss Nisbet, her spinster sister-in-law.

She went as far south west as Plymouth, where her cousin Mrs Kelly now lived with her husband. She returned to the Matchams for several months during the summer, before returning to Bath. There is no record or reference in her letters to Horatio as to how she travelled. Most likely she took the Mailcoach between London and Bath, which made the journey of 106 miles in about sixteen hours, travelling at about twelve miles per hour and changing horses every seven.

It was not until Fanny settled in Bath that she showed signs of being cheerful and at ease. Her father-in-law suggested sharing a house, and together they rented 17 New Kings Street on a three-year lease. It was small but convenient for the places of importance in Bath. There were difficulties in finding suitable servants. Bett Thurlow, their servant from Burnham, found Bath did not agree with her and "left me in the midst of it, she was dissatisfied and never content and a most wretched temper. The character of the servants in this town is I am sorry to say very bad.."

The letters written to Horatio around Christmas time reveal a contented Fanny. Many people had been kind and attentive to her; she was in good health; she had dined with Lord Hood on Christmas Day; she had met Lord and Lady Bridport and had gleaned some bits of naval news. But, alas, she was living in the false hope that her husband would be back in England within a few months.

Bath was then the most fashionable town in England and next to London was the centre of artistic importance. It had been rebuilt in a new and elegant style in the Eighteenth century, the famous Royal Crescent completed in 1775. People visited Bath to 'take the waters', not only in the restored Roman Baths but particularly in the Pump Room. It was far more than a health resort; it was a place to socialise and to circulate among the famous and fashionable, to see elegant behaviour and to participate in gaming. There were theatres and concerts to attend and days would be filled with social visiting and shopping. At night there were card parties, supper parties and balls to attend.

"Mrs F.H.N. was never in such good health as here with some cheerful neighbours ... as to myself every month in this place of warmth and ease and quietude adds something to my strength", so wrote Horatio's father to his son in August 1795. Life in Bath was anything but quiet *"I dined last night at Admiral Dickson's for the first time of my doing such a thing since we came to Bath.. card tables and all stayed for supper".*

There were many notable people whom Fanny met and who befriended her, such as Lord and Lady Howe, Sir Thomas Shelly, Lady Saumarez and others of high rank and who were connected with the navy. Her friends and the wives of naval officers visited her. Mrs Kelly, her cousin, came at times, they were close friends even though Horatio considered her selfish and odd. Fanny thrived on the praise of "My Dearest Husband". She missed him greatly, and on one occasion, having been asked to the Sheriff's Ball, she declined the invitation having *"no desire of being in a great crowd, therefore I shall not go. You cannot think how quiet I have grown..but I mean to be quite gay when I see my dearest husband and Josiah"* She was continually anxious for his safety and wondered how long he could continue so fortunate and well protected. *"I never hear the wind but my dear husband and child are fully in my thoughts, indeed they are never absent from my mind".*

In order to please Horatio Fanny had her teeth put in order and she admitted that it improved her appearance. She assured him that she never travelled by stagecoach; she tried to please him in every way despite his absence. Their letters revealed more affection for each other than had been apparent during their years together in Norfolk.

As well as news about the Nelson family, Fanny wrote about every aspect of life that was taking place around her, such as the changes in fashion *"such revolution in our dress since you left me. Now our waists are lengthened, heads dressed flat at the side, very high in front and low upon the forehead, short sleeves and some ladies showing their elbows, short petticoats, nay above the ankle with the fashionable and little or no heels to the shoes. Gloves are almost beyond the pocket of anyone, none but the long ones are in use, none less than 3 shillings a pair. The ladies of quality have a fashion in their mode of speaking, laughing or smiling at every word which I don't like".*

Wigs were going out of fashion, although the hair was covered both indoors and outdoors. The portrait of Fanny by Daniel Orme, painted in 1798, shows her wearing a bonnet which was typical of the Georgian era. Fanny had a string of pearls which Horatio had sent made into a bandeau to adorn her head and bracelets made from a chain. From the newspapers and from the general conversation Fanny was able to keep Horatio informed about the effect of the war on everyday life.

For the upper classes life changed little, as it was a period of new comforts and enlightenment; poets, painters, novelists all provided stimulation for wealth and leisure. The price of food rose and in Portsmouth and south eastern ports there was fear of invasion. The marriage between Prince William and Princess Caroline of Brunswick took place in April 1795 and Fanny related all the gossip concerning them, namely that the bride was homesick and was shown little sympathy from the bridegroom. (Horatio corresponded with Prince William giving him his account of battles and events).

The financial affairs of the Nelsons were frequently mentioned in their letters.

17 January 1795, c/o Agamemnon, St Fiorenzo *"Much as I regret being parted from you, still we must look beyond the present day and two or three months may make the difference of every comfort or otherwise to our income. I hope we may have many happy years to live together and if we can bring £2000 round I am determined to purchase some neat cottage, when we shall have occasion to change. As for Josiah I have no doubt he will be a comfort to both of us, his understanding is excellent and his disposition really good. He is a seaman every inch of him".*

Two years later Nelson's financial position was considerably improved, as well as the sum of £2304 due to him from the navy, there was almost £500 due in prize money. Hence £2000 could easily be spared for a home. "We shall be vagabonds no longer." It had been agreed that they would settle somewhere near Norwich. Fanny considered £500 was the sum necessary to furnish a home and that 'We have nothing to do with more spare bedrooms than one or two.'

Slow progress had been made towards the inheritance left to the Nelsons by John Herbert, who had died in 1793. Fanny was very dissatisfied with the infrequent communications from Mr Stanley, the Attorney General in Nevis, or Mr Baillie, her lawyer in Bristol. In 1794 she received £50 interest and bought herself a piano with half that amount, then three years later she received £450 which was interest plus annuity. By April 1797 Fanny was hopeful that all the debts and the legacy should be paid off following a shipment of 400 hogshead of sugar from the Montpelier Estate to Bristol.

She continued to be interested in Nevis and all that was happening there. Her chief informant was Captain Mills, who had recently left the Nisbet Estates to be a merchant trader between Bristol and the West Indies. She often visited the Pinneys in Bristol, who were involved in shipping having sold most of their interest in Nevis. Life in the West Indies was again precarious since the outbreak of war. British and French fleets had been sent out to Caribbean waters. The British were the superior fleet and in 1794 had captured Tobago, Martinique and St Lucia. There had been a very high incidence of Yellow Fever, accounting for the deaths of many thousands of soldiers, sailors and inhabitants of the West Indies. "All we know in Nevis are well". Martha Herbert, now Mrs Hamilton, never stirred from her house and had thirty cats; her marriage had not been happy and her only child had died in infancy. The inheritance of Montpelier passed to cousin Magnus Moreton whose wife had miscarried, thus losing a son and heir to the estate.

The sea battle fought off Cape St Vincent, at the southwest corner of Portugal, was the greatest occasion of Nelson's career at that point in time. The news reached England by the end of February 1797, as well as the announcement that Nelson was promoted to Admiral. Fanny was somewhat bewildered by all the sudden excitement and was flattered by the praise given of his conduct. "You are universally the subject of conversation". A long letter described all the people who had written to Fanny or who had spoken of his skill and intrepidity.

At a morning concert given by Colonel Glover, Baron Dillon announced Fanny's presence to the audience who all made their bow and enquired after the Admiral. "I never saw anything to elevate your father equal to this".

February 16, 1791, *"My dearest Fanny - I am most perfectly well and rich in honour as is Josiah and Hoste. It would not be right to attempt detailing the action as it comes from a much better pen than mine. God bless you and my dear father and believe me your ever most affectionate husband, Horatio Nelson".*

Josiah had been aboard the Captain and had "behaved well at St Vincent" and shortly afterwards was to be addressed as Lieutenant Nisbet. A further letter written on 3 March read "I shall come one day or other laughing home when we shall retire from the busy scene of life" but there was no indication when that day might be. In June, Fanny had received instructions to send fifty good blankets (with the letter N woven in the centre that they might not be sold) as his winter gift to Burnham. They were to be of such good quality they should last for seven years at least. That was the last letter Horatio wrote with his right hand.

On 16 August 1797 Sir John Jervis, who was Commander of the Mediterranean Fleet, wrote informing Lady Nelson that *"Sir Horatio Nelson had added very much to the laurels he had won before the assault on the town of Santa Cruz on the island of Tenerife. He is wounded but not dangerously, and I hope your Ladyship will soon be made happy by his presence in England, wither he will proceed the moment Theseus joins. I have the honour with the very great respect, your Ladyship's very faithful and obedient servant, J/Jervis"*

Using his left hand Horatio wrote to Fanny, a spidery scrawl that was hard to read, reassuring her that he was well and was soon to join her in Bath. The letter added that Josiah had been instrumental in saving his life.

It was a stroke of God's providence that Josiah had been called to Horatio's cabin to help him sort out letters from Fanny, which he wished to burn in case they fell into the hands of anyone else. After this was done he tried to dissuade Josiah from accompanying him ashore "supposing your Mother was to lose us both, what will she do?" but Josiah insisted. As Nelson was putting his foot over the boat to land ashore he was shot through the elbow, he stumbled and Josiah, laying him in the bottom of the boat, covered the wound with his hat so that his stepfather would not see the blood oozing from the wound. He then used his neckscarf to tie a tourniquet below the shoulder to stop bleeding. Five other seamen helped Nelson back to the Theseus and with difficulty got him aboard where the amputation of the severed arm took place, without anaesthesia and with not a sound from the patient during the operation.

Nelson returned home in the Seahorse arriving at Spithead on 1 September and was granted leave to strike his flag and go ashore for the recovery of his wounds. He arrived at Bath three days later.

CHAPTER SIX

THE WOUNDED HERO

There was nothing to warn Fanny of Horatio's arrival in Bath. It was a Sunday evening on September 3rd when Fanny, having returned from attending Evensong with her father-in-law and her niece Susannah, heard a horse and carriage outside the door, followed by the voice of her husband. She opened the door to see what was almost beyond her belief, the man who four years previously had been so eager to go to sea now stood before her a physical wreck.

An eminent physician, Dr Faulkner, was summoned to care for him and his wound was dressed daily by Mr Nicholls. The wound was gruesome. The area around the wound was septic. Another complication had arisen when the ship's surgeon, whilst tying the ligature above the amputated arm, inadvertently included a nerve and some muscle fibre when making the tight noose around the artery, consequently whenever his arm was tensed the severed nerve was pulled causing acute pain. For weeks the ligature would not come away. Before that happened the Nelsons moved to London staying in Bond Street where Horatio was under the care of Mr Cruikshank.Two surgeons examined him with a view to assessing the need for a further operation but this was decided against. The ligature came away at the end of November, following which the wound healed quickly and the pain and the suffering ceased.

Fanny was in constant attention upon his every need, dressing the wound, feeding him, helping him to dress and helping him to use his left arm and hand as much as he could. A special one-piece knife and fork was made for him so that he could eat more easily. Whenever he wore his jacket the empty sleeve of his right arm had to be pinned across his chest. Horatio not only suffered physically but was often in a state of depression. He had lost some of his self confidence, his pride had suffered fearing the action at Santa Cruz was a mistake and feared he might not go to sea again, that he was a burden as well as useless in the service to his country. He related to Fanny the happenings at Calvi when he had lost the sight of his eye, which had not been removed though he had no sight in it. Josiah was often the subject of their conversation, how he had saved his Father's life together with the coxswain John Sykes. For this brief period in their lives their roles were reversed, Horatio dependent on Fanny who greatly admired his power of physical endurance and mental resilience. The Naval attack on Santa Cruz had been a disaster but his conduct during the attack had been officially approved and his success at the Battle of St Vincent had made him a hero. He was revered, loved and respected by his countrymen, rich and poor. This was not just because of his brilliance but because he showed to the men who served under him, humanity and understanding.. He understood their needs and helped to improve the living conditions of the crews. No sailors ever mutinied who served under him.

Most of Horatio's leave was spent in London where he was able to undertake some activities during the day. At Christmas time they joined their father in Bath for a family reunion. His eldest brother Maurice was still employed at the Navy Office, the Rector was always trying to make use of Horatio's position to gain promotion in the church. Neither of his brothers-in-law were respected by him, George Matcham was continually moving from one grand house to another, and Thomas Bolton had fathered seven children in quick succession. Josiah had not returned on leave but had been given promotion and was now in command of the Dolphin, a hospital ship, he seemed to be making progress in his naval career.

Honours were bestowed on Admiral Nelson, he attended a levee at St James Palace and was officially presented to King George 111 and afterwards invested as Knight of the Bath. He received the Freedom of the City of London and of the City of Bath. A special Service of Thanks for the many mercies bestowed upon him was held in St George's Church in Hanover Square. Profuse and heartfelt thanks were offered by a large congregation none more so than Fanny.

Their financial position was put in order, he received Rear Admiral's pay, he had collected prize money and received a disability pension of £1,000 a year. A neat cottage was now a certainty. A suitable house in Suffolk, near Ipswich was recommended by Sam Bolton, and was bought at an Auction for £2,000. Only a brief visit to see their home, Round Wood, was made before the purchase was completed. It was to be Fanny's duty to furnish it during Horatio's next period of service.

The Admiralty and particularly Sir John Jervis, who had now been created Earl St Vincent, were anxious for Nelson to rejoin the fleet. England had lost control at sea, trade was suffering and the whole of Europe was under threat from Napoleon. Nelson was equally keen to return to sea since his recovery, he hated the French and Napoleon in particular. "Duty is the great business of a sea officer, all private considerations give way to it." This had always been Nelson's maxim.

He was now given command of the Vanguard. Once again Fanny faced the prospect of life without a husband. They had been happy together during the past months. He openly acknowledged the debt he owed her for his recovery and their friends and family had observed their mutual show of affection and consideration towards each other. Fanny remained in London when Nelson departed to join the Vanguard at Portsmouth on the 29th March 1798.

CHAPTER SEVEN

ROUND WOOD - THE NEAT COTTAGE

From the day of Nelson's departure to Portsmouth nothing went well with Fanny. She was blamed that numerous chattels could not be found amongst his baggage. Silk stockings, lost linen, black stock (neckwear), muckabout towels, keys. Neither did her list of items tally with Nelson's own. She was full of abject apologies in her letters and miserable herself, imagining her one armed husband trying to manage with the help of a seemingly useless new servant.

His complaints and her oversight marred their parting, although there were words of affection in a letter from Horatio. *"From my heart I wish it were peace then not a moment would I lose in getting to my cottage"* ...

April 7th 1798, "The wind is fair and we are getting under sail and I pray to God to bless you and soon send us peace when believe me nothing in this world can exceed the pleasure I shall have in returning to you". Neither of these aspirations was fulfilled. He never spent a night in their 'neat cottage' and his return to Fanny was brief and disastrous.

Round Wood was the first real home that the Nelsons could call their own. It was a simple and plain gentleman's residence which was considered by Fanny to be large enough for the present. It had two parlours and four bedrooms, kitchen, dairy, cellar and wine vaults. Outside there was a large barn, stables and a cow house. There were 50 acres of good arable land which surrounded the house which were let to a tenant. The nearest hamlet was Wix Ufford and nearest market town was Ipswich.

Fanny moved into the house in May together with her father-in law. She had bought furniture and carpets in London and other items had been stored in Bath. Improvements were needed both inside and outside the house, shutters had to be made and damp patches on the inside walls patched up. The well had to be deepened and the pump repaired. The wine cellars were filled with the casks of wine Horatio had been given by the Spanish Governor of Santa Cruz, the wines had to be properly bottled, Fanny wanted them kept in good condition until Horatio's return. Three servants were engaged for domestic work and two men for outdoor tasks.

The first summer there was a fine one, the crops were good and Fanny had various improvements made in the garden and trees were planted around the house as a shelter against the cruel winter winds. A gardener who worked nearby raised carnations (Fanny's favourite flower). He had named his most recent plant Lord Nelson so two layers were bought at ten shillings and sixpence each, an extravagance that was thought justifiable. Although Horatio had told his wife that 'money was trash' Fanny was very economical, she complained that the housekeeping was expensive even though they dined off cold roast beef, not being able to procure fish or fowl.

Only occasional visits were made to Ipswich which was a quiet place with little trade or business. A big contrast to Bath or London. Soldiers were stationed around the town and county in case of invasion. A post chaise was hired rather than Fanny owning one. Most of her time was spent indoors, in the parlour where a recent portrait of Horatio was hung, it was a true likeness of him which had been painted by Lemuel Abbot. Prints of this were much in demand. She told him in her letters that gazing at his portrait gave her a feeling of closeness to him during his absence.

Many people called on her and she dutifully returned their calls. Several of the neighbours lived in style but Fanny never forced herself into titled company and disliked some who called themselves 'ladies'. Her closest friends were the Middletons, Captain and Mrs Bouche and old Admiral Reeve whom she regarded as a fif fad. Only occasionally did she attend dinners or balls, the events during Race Week at Ipswich included two balls but she appeared to have neither the inclination nor the strength to socialise.

Horatio wrote advising her "But my dear Fanny, unless you can game and talk scandal, that is lies, most probably your company will never be coveted by county tabbies, young people have more goodness than old age". She probably knew she was humdrum and only in her letters to him did she reveal her true feelings and her thoughts.

Her greatest friend was Mrs Berry who was a frequent guest at Round Wood. Captain Berry had served with Nelson since 1796 and Josiah had served under him. She helped to make curtains and other furnishings for the house, they shared many interests and had the same opinions concerning indecency and insobriety. Her father was her constant companion except when he made visits to Bath. The Bolton family lived nearby and were also frequent visitors. The twin daughters, Kitty and Susannah were regarded as bad tempered and needed to be made nicer in many ways. When the Rector came to stay two rooms had to be made available for his needs. When Suckling came to stay he was taken ill and had to be nursed by Fanny.

Letters from Horatio took many weeks to arrive and came infrequently. Fanny spent the time in a state of anticipation, awaiting news of him and the hope of his return July 16th 1798, *"My dear Husband, I only write to tell you of my extreme anxiety to hear from you, no one period of war have I felt more than I do at this moment. I really am so affected that it has enervated me*

ON THIS SITE STOOD
MONTPELIER HOUSE
WHEREIN
ON THE 11TH DAY OF MARCH 1787
HORATIO NELSON
OF IMMORTAL MEMORY
THEN CAPTAIN OF H.M.S. BOREAS
WAS MARRIED TO
FRANCES HERBERT NISBET

beyond description, still I think all will turn out to your sanguine wishes, I hope in God it will. The papers tell us you have been in Naples, but was not satisfied and immediately sailed for Malta. I wish I knew that Josiah was with you. A line from him would do me good, I can only hope that his duty to his professions and his love for you employ his time. I am one of the old fashioned mothers and think there is something called natural affection. I am sure I feel it for him..."

Nelson's wishes and the orders he received were to seek out and destroy the French Navy, whose position in the Mediterranean was not known. He had a squadron of ten 'seventy fours' and one fifty gun ship. They sailed for Toulon, where before they intercepted the French, a violent storm had struck the British ships including the Vanguard. Several days of delay gave the French fleet the opportunity to sail eastwards, north of Corsica and towards Italy. Nelson suspected the possibility of Napoleon heading for Egypt and thence via the Red Sea to the British possessions in India. He therefore sailed towards Alexandria in the eastern Mediterranean.

There was no sight of the enemy at the end of June, so Nelson now proceeded northwards and westwards to ascertain that neither Crete nor the Kingdom of the two Sicilies had been captured. A month later information reached him that the enemy had sailed past a port in northern Greece, which convinced Nelson that Napoleon would be making for Alexandria. This was affirmed when the French fleet was sighted at anchor at the mouth of the Nile in Aboukir Bay.

Napoleon had already landed, advanced on Cairo and defeated the army of the Turkish rulers of Egypt. Nelson's plan was to attack the superior French line by concentrating two divisions on either side of what was thought to be the impregnable line, while a third division was to attack the transports.

47

The British went into action at 5.40 p.m. on 1st August and by 9pm the fighting was over. The French fleet was in disarray, having been attacked from the shore side when their guns were facing seawards. Half of their ships had been shattered and the two remaining enemy ships fled. Nelson's tactics had been highly successful. His 'band of brothers,' who had each known their special duties, had all fought valiantly and use had been made of attacking at dusk.

The Battle of the Nile was a humiliating defeat for the French. Napoleon's hopes of marching to India were abandoned and the British were now in complete control of the Mediterranean. Recognition and rewards were piled upon the hero; he was made a Peer of the Realm and was promoted to Rear Admiral of the Red, being voted £2,000 for his lifetime and that of two of his successors. The Turkish Sultan sent him fabulous gifts, as did the Czar of Russia and the East India Company voted him a gift of £10,000.

The official dispatches did not arrive in London until October 1st. When the news was announced the celebrations which followed were tremendous both in London and all over the country. Church bells were rung, ships in port were dressed 'over-all', there were firework displays, special plays performed, songs composed. There was no limit to the praise for the 'Hero of the Nile'.

The newspapers tormented Fanny, wanting news which she was unable and unwilling to give. The first dispatch after the battle had been sent with the husband of her friend, Captain Berry, on the ship Leander but this ship was captured by the enemy's ship Le Genereaux. A further dispatch was sent by Captain Capel, who sailed to Naples and then travelled overland to London. He also brought with him a letter from Horatio to Fanny

... "I am thank God much better than expected and I hope I will make Europe happy in the certain destruction of the French Army. The people of the country

48

are rising up against them every hour, such are the fruits of our conquest. Victory is certainly not a name strong enough for such a scene as I have passed. I shall probably be in England in November but more of this hereafter. With kindest love to my father and all our friends. Believe me ever your most affectionate husband, Horatio Nelson."

In Ipswich a special ball was held and a supper given in honour of the hero's wife, bands played and people danced to the tune of 'Lady Nelson's Fancy'. Round Wood had many callers, people of rank who had not previously troubled to make themselves known. Letters poured in from friends and well wishers, one from her Nisbet sister-in-law describing the celebration which had taken place in Glasgow....Fanny was disappointed that Horatio had only been created a Baron, whereas St Vincent had received an Earldom and Duncan a Viscountcy. Both of these Admirals had played a less significant part than Nelson had in the recent battle, but Nelson was not a Commander-in-Chief and, therefore, had to put up with less honours than his superiors. Prime Minister William Pitt explained in the House of Commons that as Nelson had won the greatest naval victory on record this was a far greater honour than being made an Earl or a Viscount.

Fanny was now included among the principal female nobility and gentry moving in court circles. Her first presentation at the Court of St James was on 23rd November 1798, when the Countess of Chatham presented her to the Queen. The following summer she was invited to 'The Queen's Drawing Room' to a reception in honour of the King's birthday.

According to the Morning Star, Lady Nelson was splendidly attired in a superb robe of silver, ornamented to correspond - a beautiful headdress with an elegant plume of ostrich feathers.' She was well received in Court, she found it easy to talk to the King and Queen. whom she liked very much. Fanny possessed all the graces and the charm necessary to circulate with Royalty. The Walpoles, who owned a large house in London as well as their estates in Norfolk, were very attentive to Fanny, helping her to follow all the correct procedures. In the following year she again paid her respects at Court and was made welcome by their Royal Highnesses. On this occasion, for the sake of economy, she made a point of attending Court before the spring thus avoiding having to buy an entire new outfit.

Most of the winter of 1798 was spent in Bath, Fanny suffering from fatigue and a troublesome cough. The winters in Suffolk were cold and wet the roads impassable and social life ceased; in Bath she renewed friendships and her health improved. Returning to Round Wood in the following spring with her father-in-law she was much occupied sorting out domestic difficulties, her financial affairs and receiving countless visitors. Her responsibilities seemed to overwhelm her. Her in-laws were constantly making demands on her and expecting favours. The Rector (The Reverend William Nelson) was hoping for promotion in the church and a better style of living as well as aspiring to be Horatio's heir. His pride and selfishness upset his father as well as Fanny. Friends often asked her to recommend their offspring, who were serving in the Navy, for promotion. Naval officers brought her first hand news of Horatio which she welcomed though on some occasions she was moved to tears in their presence and had to excuse herself from the room. During that year 1799 Suckling Nelson died causing much grief among all the family. She continued to write regularly to Horatio, his letters came less and less frequently. A house in St James street London was rented for the winter, it was convenient for both her father and her to be there. She consulted a physician about her health, she wanted to be fully restored to health before Horatio's return, but when recommended that she should go to Lisbon to escape the winter, she declined to commit herself before obtaining her husband's consent even though she yearned for the sun and warmth. Instead she clothed herself in two suits of flannel. She had friends and many callers in London; the house was too small for relatives to stay, only her niece came, the Rector's daughter, who was attending a school in Chelsea. Her cousin Martha from Nevis had bought a house in Harley street, so she was able to gather news about Nevis and was told how proud her friends there were to have known the 'hero of the Nile'.

The new century was welcomed in without news of Horatio's return. His imminent return had been expected since before Christmas. He had told Fanny that Lisbon was a dreadful place and gave her no encouragement to change climates, nor to visit him in Naples. Their father became very ill, it was nearly a month before he showed signs of recovery. At least in London they were able to consult London doctors instead of being at the mercy of country 'butchers'. She had to forgo all social activities until his recovery in early March when the old man had enough strength to have his portrait painted by Sir William Beechey. In a letter she wrote to Horatio she was able to tell him that *"Our good father has been in good spirits since we last heard from you. Indeed my spirits are quite worn out, the time has been so long. I thank God for the preservation of my dear husband and your recent success off Malta. God bless you my dear husband and grant us a happy meeting."*

51

CHAPTER EIGHT

NEWS FROM NAPLES

Horatio Nelson lost the sight of his right eye at Calvi. He had lost his right arm in the Battle of Tenerife and in Naples he lost his heart to Lady Hamilton. He fell in love helplessly and hopelessly. He was helpless in resisting the beautiful, seductive and manipulative being who found in him passion and mutual sexual fulfilment. It was hopeless for Fanny because the love her husband had for Emma Hamilton was to surpass all his previous loves and infatuations.

Following the Battle of the Nile Nelson sailed towards Naples. It was a large and important city situated in the central Mediterranean and the capital of the Kingdom of the two Sicilies, under the rule of the Bourbon monarchy. By going to Naples Nelson was obeying orders to assist King Ferdinand against the threat of a French invasion.

Having sustained an injury in the head at the Battle of Aboukir Bay, Nelson was feeling sick and weary. News of his victory had not yet reached England and he did not know how the news would be received. The Vanguard was in need of repair and Naples had a good dockyard. As he sailed into Naples on the 22nd September 1798 he received a tumultuous welcome. A flotilla of five hundred boats, including the King's barge, filled the bay, all flying flags and streamers.

Foremost amongst those who boarded Vanguard were Sir William Hamilton, the British Minister in Naples, and his wife Lady Hamilton, who fainted into the arms of the hero a few minutes before King Ferdinand came on board welcoming 'Nostra Liberatore'. Both the Hamiltons welcomed their famous guest into their home, the luxurious Palazzo Sessa, which overlooked the bay with the scenic Mount Vesuvius in the background. Nelson was still suffering from his wound and needed rest and recuperation. Emma 'mothered' him, bathing his aching head with asses milk, soothing away his aches and pains. Sir William and he engaged in intellectual conversations and Horatio took great interest in his host's collection of volcanic specimens, his pictures and his precious ornaments. He was introduced by Emma to the Queen, Maria Carolina and King Ferdinand.

Fortune had again favoured Horatio when he sailed into the Bay of Naples. There he was in his element, he gained power and fame, he lost his inhibitions, and flattery was showered upon him, especially by Emma. He needed Sir William not only as a highly intelligent friend but to speak French for him at Court.

The threesome were interdependent upon each other and became known as the 'Tria Juncta in Uno'. Sir William provided a cover for what later became an intimate affair between his wife and his guest. Despite her hero's appearance, one eye half closed and one arm missing, Emma regarded this little man as her ultimate prize, to be captured and manipulated for her own ends and to further the cause of her friends the Bourbons. Sir William was grateful for Horatio's support in the last days of his diplomatic career, so let the relationship develop without interference.

In a letter to Fanny in October 1798, Horatio described, as far as he was able, the celebrations and honours that the Neapolitans showered upon him *"Our time here is spent in business and what is called pleasure. I am not my own master for five minutes"* he quoted some of the songs composed 'beyond what I ever could deserve' but above all he described his close friendship with the Hamiltons.

53

"My pride is being your husband, the son of my father and in having Sir William and Lady Hamilton for my friends ... I hope to have the pleasure of introducing you to Lady Hamilton. She is one of the best women in the world, how few could have made the turn she has. She is an honour to her sex and a proof that even reputation may be regained, but I owe it requires a great soul... May God bless you my dear Fanny and give us in due time a happy meeting. Should the King grant me a peerage I believe I scarcely need state the propriety of you going to court..."

The Hamiltons and Nelson met briefly in September 1793, when Nelson was sent on an urgent diplomatic mission to King Ferdinand to plead for troops to reinforce the defence of Toulon, which was being held by a small French Royalist army. Following that occasion Horatio had written to Fanny giving an account of his meeting with the King and the Hamiltons,

'Lady Hamilton has been wonderfully kind and good to Josiah. She is a young woman of amiable manners and who does honour to the station to which she is raised.'

Fanny knew the brief facts about Lady Hamilton's past, that she came from a poor family in the north, that she was very beautiful and had put her talents to good use. That she had been the mistress of Sir Harry Featherstonaugh in Sussex and later Sir Charles Grenville had become her protector. The artist George Romney had been overawed by her beauty, painting several portraits of her. Sir William Hamilton a widower, was also overawed by her beauty. He was the established Ambassador in Naples. Through an extraordinary transaction he acquired Emma from his nephew Sir Charles Grenville. She arrived in Naples with her mother in 1796 and since then had married Sir William, who was thirty years older than her. She had played an important part in the Naples Court as the confidante of Queen Carolina. She was known still to still have a northern accent, to have retained her beauty and to be vivacious and amusing. Fanny had been told of her dramatic activities, performing 'attitudes', soliloquies, dressed in flowing garments, expressing a variety of postures and moods. She doubted that she would find any common interest with this woman.

At long last a letter from Horatio contained news of Josiah. He had arrived in Naples in command of a sloop, Bonne Citoyenne, in September. He was now eighteen and had been in the navy for six years. It seemed that his career was not making the progress that had been hoped for. He arrived in Naples carrying a letter from his Commander, St Vincent, telling Horatio that *"Josiah loves drink and low company and is thoroughly ignorant of all forms of service, inattentive, obstinate and wrongheaded beyond measure and had he not been your step son he would have been annihilated months ago. With all this he is honest and truth telling and I dare say will if you ask him subscribe to every word I have written."*

Fanny was not given all the details of this letter but for Horatio it was a great disappointment. He tried to defend Josiah but if he could not live up to the expectations his father had for him he was no longer prepared to support him. Josiah was reported to be drunk at the famous party Emma gave to celebrate Horatio's fortieth birthday, and drunkenness was abhorred by Nelson. Horatio wrote to Fanny on 17th January 1799 *"I wish I could say much to you and my satisfaction about Josiah but I am sorry to say with real grief that there is nothing good about him, he must sooner or later be broke, but I am sure neither you nor I can help it."*

To Fanny's consternation he also wrote that if Josiah remained under Lady Hamilton's care for six months she could fashion him in spite of himself and make something of all his bluntness. Josiah rarely wrote to his mother and he may have considered it disloyal and hurtful to inform her of her husband's flirtatious behaviour. Several years later he told her that he had neither respect nor any affection for Emma.

A letter from Lady Hamilton to Lady Nelson written in December 1798 was full of flattery of Horatio and telling her of the delight at being able to care for Lord Nelson, adding that *"Josiah is so much improved in every respect. We are delighted with him. He is an excellent officer, very steady with one of the best hearts in the world. I love him very much and although we quarrel sometimes he loves me and does as I would have him...."*

Josiah did not remain under Emma's influence for long. In April 1799 he took command of the Thalia. By now his step-father felt he had been spoilt and that more had been done for him, pointing out how conspicuous he was as well as being envied, beseeching him not to let his parents down and assuring him of the love they both had for him.

The wayward officer tried to make amends, but his resolution to improve himself did not last long. When the Thalia was sent to Leghorn in May 1799 Josiah smashed up a privateer for firewood. Within the next twelve months he had quarrelled with one of his officers, put the ship's surgeon under arrest and told the ship's master to jump overboard. Finally, in October 1800, after a short spell on convoy duty he was sent home on leave on half pay.

It had been the intention of Lord Nelson to return home not later than May 1799. He had instructed Fanny to buy a bigger house than Round Wood. *"If we have enough money a neat house near Hyde Park in London, but on no account the other side of Portman Square, I detest Baker Street, in short do as you please, you know my wishes and income. A neat carriage I desire you will order and if possible get some good servants. You will take care that I am not let down".* He also explained that *"the poor Queen has again made me promise not to quit her and her family till prospects appear brighter than they do at present."*

His letters came rarely and were brief. She was kept informed of his whereabouts and some of his activities. Having received his Peerage he now signed his letters simply 'Nelson'. Fanny knew that Horatio sailed to Leghorn with a cargo of Neapolitan troops in November 1798. She also knew that due to the French advance on Naples on 24th December 1799 Horatio had evacuated the Royal Family and the Hamiltons, taking them to Palermo on the island of Sicily onboard Vanguard. A terrifying storm had blown

up, ripping the sails and cracking a mast. The Royal Family were sick and ill, their six year old son died of convulsions during the voyage in the arms of Lady Hamilton. They remained at Palermo 'dragging an existence from day to day.' Horatio assured her how dreadful it would have been for her if she attempted to join him in either Naples or Palermo.

What was not known was that at Palermo her husband was on the one hand suffering from headaches and depression due to the fall of Naples, and on the other hand he was even more in love with Emma. The flattery, the flirting and the friendliness developed into a physical relationship which dominated them both and which was to last for the remainder of their lives. They were discreet in their lovemaking, giving no reason for members of the household to be offended by their behaviour and avoiding suspicions from outside.

Horatio's loyalty was now divided between restoring the Bourbons to their throne (thus pleasing Emma) and his duties to the Navy, who required him to intercept the French fleet in the Mediterranean. In June 1799 he was transferred to command the Foundroyant. Lord Keith had succeeded Lord St Vincent as

Commander in Chief and both their Lordships were highly critical of Nelson when, by returning to Naples, he had ignored orders to sail for Minorca. The Bourbon monarchy was restored to Naples but as the situation was still unstable in Sicily Nelson returned there. On his return to Palermo in August he was created Duke of Bronte and given a Sicilian estate in honour of his services to their country.

Lord Keith felt that Nelson was obsessed with the importance of preserving Sicily and was committing a grave error in his behaviour and had brought discredit upon himself. Some references to Nelson's social life were reported in the English newspapers, which were read by Fanny. She always had disliked the press and insinuated in one her letters that certain people were jealous of him and anxious to criticise him. She did not want to believe anything wrong about him, believing in his goodness. She knew that there had been other women in his life before they met. He had told her about the amiable Mrs Moutray whom he met on Antigua, where her husband was the Admiralty's Resident Commissioner and that she had made his life in the 'hell hole' bearable. He had remained friendly with her after her return to England when she had been widowed.

In Quebec in 1782, when he was serving onboard the Albermere, he was so enamoured with a sixteen-year old that he nearly resigned his commission in order to remain in Quebec and marry her. The girl had shown no response to his attentions so he remained in the service. A year later when in France on six months leave he fell in love with a girl he hardly knew in St Omer, who was staying there with her clerical father. She also rejected his offer of marriage; another romantic encounter was over.

What his wife was never told was that in 1794, whilst refitting the Agamemnon in Leghorn, he had a promiscuous affair with a Frenchwoman of great beauty, Adelaide Correglia. She was referred to as Nelson's 'dolly'. The affair continued for almost a year. Few, if any, of his fellow officers thought much of this, it being understood that once past Gibraltar, marriage vows could be left behind.

Early in 1800 the situation in the Mediterranean had again become serious after Bonaparte was reported to have escaped from Egypt, had reached France and become First Consul. Lord Keith and Nelson met at Leghorn and sailed together from there to Malta, where Nelson was left in charge of the blockade. He again returned to Palermo, on the excuse of his ill health, wanting to see Emma and to visit his newly acquired estate of Bronte.

The patience of Lords Keith and Spencer was exhausted and they ordered Nelson's return to England forthwith where he would be more likely to recover his health and strength "than in an inactive situation in a foreign court, however pleasing the respect and gratitude shown for your services might be". His request to return to England using a naval vessel and taking the Hamiltons with him was not granted. Sir William was retiring from his post and returning to England. Despite the fact that French troops were in northern Italy, increasing the hazards of a journey across Europe, it was decided that 'the trio' should return overland.

Lord Nelson struck his flag in July 1800, signifying his temporary resignation from the service. Fanny was told 'you must expect to find me a worn and old man' as Horatio had recently lost some of his front teeth. He now signed his letters Bronte Nelson of the Nile. The party planned to arrive in mid October in London, where Nelson wanted a house and looked forward to a happy meeting. Queen Carolina had been persuaded to travel as far as Vienna with the trio. The triumphal party consisted of fourteen carriages and two large baggage waggons, led by the Queen, her family and attendants, followed the next day by the English party which included Emma's mother and a friend Miss Knight.

Sir William was seriously ill by the time they reached Vienna, where they remained for a month. They stayed in hotels en route and were entertained and feted by a variety of notable people. They arrived in Prague, then proceeded to Dresden. They took a boat to convey them on the River Elbe towards Prussia, Magdeburg and thence to Hamburg, spending at least a week there. There were several reports describing either Nelson or Emma. In Vienna Lady Minto thought that Horatio "had not altered in the least, the same simple manners, but he is devoted to Emma, he thinks her quite an angel" Lord Fitzharris commented that "we never sat down to dinner less than sixty or seventy persons ... Lady Hamilton is without exception the most coarse, ill mannered, disagreeable woman we met with".

At Dresden they put up at the Great Hotel and dined with the English Ambassador, Mr Elliott. In Dresden at that time Mrs St George was invited to the Embassy. Her sharp tongue gave further account of Emma "she is bold, forward, coarse, assuming and vain. Her figure is colossal, but excepting for her feet which are hideous, well shaped. Her bones are large and she is exceedingly enbonpoint ...Lord Nelson is a little man without any dignity, Lady Hamilton takes possession of him and he is a willing captive, the most submissive and devoted I have seen. Sir William is old, infirm and never spoke a word to-day but to applaud her". The cost of their journey amounted to well over £3,000 for Nelson, who divided the bills with Sir William.

A frigate had been requested to take them from Hamburg back to England but only a packet, the King George, was provided. They arrived at Yarmouth in November 1800. Flags were flying and bells were rung, the horses were taken from their coach and the fishermen pulled the coach to the nearest inn. They drove to Round Wood, not far away, where they found the house empty.

Nelson had overlooked the fact that he had instructed Fanny to await him in London. Two days later they arrived in London, where Fanny and his father had been expecting them for several weeks. The reunion took place at St Neots Hotel, Kings Street, St James. The house they were to rent in Dover Street was not yet ready for their occupation. They were in the hall when his Grace the Duke of Queensberry paid a visit, staying about an hour. At five o'clock Lord and Lady Nelson and Sir William and Lady Hamilton dined together. At half past seven Lord Nelson went in a chariot to Earl Spencer, where there was a select party all evening. Lady Nelson paid a friendly visit to Countess Spencer. The Hamiltons went to a house in Grosvenor Square.

This was not the happy reunion that Fanny had looked forward to for nearly two years. Neither was her impression of Lady Hamilton at all favourable. Was this really the woman her husband had described as being one of the best women in the world? Her appearance did not indicate that she was an honour to her sex and her manners, as seen so far, and she did not appear particularly amiable. The prospect of having to become friendly with Sir William and Lady Hamilton did not please Fanny.

CHAPTER NINE

THE SEPARATION

Signs of disharmony between the Nelsons were soon apparent. Lord Nelson's time was occupied by official functions. He was presented at Court, where he was received coolly by the King. At the Lord Mayor's Procession he was cheered and mobbed by the crowds. He took his seat in the House of Lords, introduced by Lords Romsey and Grenville. His portrait was painted again by Lemual Abbott, with his chest bedecked with stars and medals and ribbons. He was rarely alone with Fanny, making a point of avoiding her unless they were bidden to be present together, such as at the Queen's Drawing Room Party on November 13th, when Sir William Hamilton was also present, without Lady Hamilton. When Countess Spencer gave a dinner party for them both she was appalled by the contempt Nelson showed his wife, who was so distressed that she retired from the table in tears. Two years previously he had shown much affection and attention to her and praised her for his recovery.

The Herald newspaper gave a description of the Nelsons and Hamiltons attending Covent Garden Theatre together. 'The whole audience burst into loud applause when Lord Nelson appeared and bowed deeply again and again; Rule Britannia was sung with gusto by the audience. Lady Nelson was dressed in white with a violet satin headdress and small white feathers. Her ladyship's person is of very pleasing description, her features are handsome and exceedingly interesting and in general her appearance is at once prepossessing and elegant. Lady Hamilton is rather 'en bon point' but her person is never the less highly graceful and her face extremely pretty. She wore a blue satin gown and a head-dress with a fine plume of feathers'

The last time that Fanny and Horatio were seen together in public was on the 24th November when, together with the Hamiltons and others, they went to see Sheridan's 'Pizarro' at the Drury Lane Theatre. The main character in the play is the evil Peruvian conqueror. The words of the heroine Elvira in the third act were too much for Fanny to bear. They were so close to her own feelings towards Horatio that she lost control of her emotions, crying out loudly before fainting. The curtain fell and Fanny was helped out of the box by Emma and her father-in-law whilst Horatio sat motionless until the end of the performance. The heat generated by the large crowd in the theatre was blamed for Lady Nelson's indisposition. She recovered sufficiently to resume her seat 'and to the great satisfaction of all present remained in the box during the rest of the performance'.

In late November the Nelsons moved into a furnished house, 15 Dover Street which Alexander Davison had found for them and were joined there by their father, Nelson was rarely present, husband and wife were leading separate lives. Behaviour which had been acceptable in Naples was not acceptable in London society who started to avoid him. There were some people who wondered whether the injury Nelson had sustained at Aboukir Bay had affected his brain causing a change in his personality. Nearly all the London newspapers, The Times, the Morning Herald, the Morning Post all taunted Lady Hamilton with her past and the fact that she was not received at court. The fashionable Morning Post wrote that 'Lady Hamilton had arrived only in the nick of time'. Only a few thousands of people read the newspapers, to the populace Nelson was their hero who could do no wrong, many thousands could not read newspapers. Fanny now realised that the rumours she had heard and read about Nelson when he was in Naples were true, and that the saying 'salt water and absence wash away love 'was also true. She loved her husband, and his father who she called 'our Father' and her son Josiah...She also realised that Emma was pregnant with Nelson's child, and that she was no longer loved. At Christmas time Fanny was left on her own whilst Nelson joined the Hamiltons for a house party at Fonthill as guests of William Beckford, a notorious dilettante. The party lasted several days during which time Emma entertained the company with performances of her 'attitudes' and dramatic soliloquises.

In the new year, 1801, Nelson was promoted to Admiral of the Blue and was given the flagship San Joseph, to be second in command of the Channel fleet. He had become gloomy and depressed and was in financial difficulties; he badly wanted to escape from the domestic dilemma and no longer needed Fanny with her gentility and her elegance and her graces. She was now the personification of his frustration standing between everything he most desired, Emma was now vital to his whole existence. He longed to go to sea again.

The details of their final parting are difficult to verify. After his return from Fonthill, living under the same roof had become unbearable for them both. Fanny objected strongly to having the Hamiltons as constant companions. Nelson would not hear a bad word spoken against Emma, claiming that he was under a great obligation to her and could only speak of her with affection and admiration. A conversation between them took place along those lines after which Fanny stormed out of the room. Nelson's solicitor, William Hazelwood related the incident but not until many years later. It was unlike Fanny to have behaved in such an impetuous manner; it was more in keeping with her husband's character. It was the last time they saw each other.

Fanny was now on her own; rather than remain in London she went to Brighton for the next two months. She invited the Rector's wife to join her there, but the invitation was turned down. Already the Nelson family were avoiding Fanny in favour of Emma. Instead she was joined by a friend Miss Locker, whose father had been a friend of Nelson's but who had recently died. It was an unsuitable place for them both, there was nothing cheerful about the greyness of the sea or the pebbled beach. Nothing soothed her feelings, searching for reasons why she had caused Nelson to desert her, feeling guilty, and pondering how she could gain his affection once again. In the past he had believed in morality and self discipline and now he was openly flaunting his own indiscretion. What was her future to be, divorce was a most complicated and expensive procedure involving annulment by Act of Parliament? Formal separations rarely took place, infidelities and children born out of wedlock occurred in all walks of life.

Nelson had left London to join his ship, having packed his clothes and made arrangements for provisions and personal possessions to be sent to Plymouth where Captain Hardy was already awaiting him. He wrote several letters to Fanny whilst she was in Brighton. These mainly complained about missing items including a key and half his wardrobe, not to mention the wrong set of decanters and tableware. In one letter he wrote, *"I only regret that I desired any person to order things for me. I could have done all in ten minutes and for a 10th part of the expense, but never mind I eat off yellow ware plate. It is too late now to send half my wardrobe, as I know not what is to become of me, nor do I care. Yours truly. Nelson."*

Before he sailed he had written to the Hamiltons giving them draft codicil to his will. Letters also passed between Emma and Mrs W. Nelson. A reference was made to Fanny, *"Tom Titt may go to the devil for all I care,"* Emma's interest in Josiah was somewhat changed from what she had professed in Naples. *"Febuary 26. The Cub is to have a frigate, the Thalia, the Earl gives it,' tis settled. So I suppose he will be up in a day or so. I only hope he will not come near me. If he does, not at home will be the answer. Am glad he is going.*" A few weeks later Josiah dined with the Hamiltons but no one asked how his Mother was. Emma had always had a jealous nature and could not tolerate a rival. She gave Fanny the nickname Tom Titt because of her small mincing step and to Josiah she gave the name the Cub.

Nelson was transferred to the St George. In March he joined Admiral Parker at Yarmouth before sailing to the Baltic. The Battle of Copenhagen took place on 2nd April and an Armistice with Denmark signed on 9th April. The following month Nelson, succeeded Parker as Commander in chief and was created Viscount Nelson of the Nile and Burnham Thorpe, as well, as Bronte which prompted Lady Nelson to take the title of Duchess of Bronte. Viscount Nelson took his seat in the House of Lords on October. In March 1802 Fanny received a letter from Alexander Davison informing her that she was to receive a settlement of £2,000 a year subject to tax amounting to £1,800 neat money. Every bill that was owing prior to Nelson's departure to sea was to be paid for by him. The sum of £4,000 which Fanny had inherited from John Herbert was to be disposed by her will. She was adequately provided for.

Davison was a close friend of Nelson. They had met in Quebec in 1782 and it was Davison who dissuaded him from attempting to marry his first love, the American girl, Mary Simpson. Davison had been a government agent, he had become very wealthy over the years; he was a financier and as such acted for Nelson as sole agent for his prize money. After Nelson's death Davison kept letters and memorabilia which have only recently (July 2002) become known, having been kept for nearly two centuries by descendants of his. Among these letters are many from Fanny, revealing how desperately she tried to woo her husband back to her, using Davison as her go-between. She became physically ill for a short time and lost what little confidence she had. These 72 letters now shed a new light on Fanny and perhaps may arouse some sympathy for her from some of Nelson's biographers.

When Fanny received this letter she consulted her brother-in-law Maurice who told her to ignore it as his brother seemed to have 'forgot himself'! In April Nelson wrote from the St George to Davison *"You will, at a proper time, and before my arrival in England signify to Lady Nelson that I expect, and for which I have made such a liberal allowance to her to be left to myself, and without any inquiries from her: for sooner than live the unhappy life I did when I last came to England, I would stay abroad for ever. My mind is fixed as fate: therefore you will send my determination in any way you may judge proper; and believe me ever your obliged and faithful friend. Nelson and Bronte."*

In Nelson's final letter to Fanny, what she considered her letter of dismissal, he wrote, *"I have done ALL I could for Josiah and done my duty as an honest and generous man and neither wish for anybody to care what becomes of me, whether I return or am left in the Baltic, seeing I have done all in my power for you and if dead, you will find I have done the same, therefore my only wish is to be left to myself and wishing you every happiness, believe me I am your affectionate Nelson and Bronte."*

In response to the pleas that Fanny was sending to Davison she received a letter from him in June, *"I hardly need to repeat how happy I should have been to have seen him with you, the happiest, his heart is so pure and good that I flatter myself that he can never be divested from his affection. I have no right to doubt it."* This was all false optimism. Fanny made two further attempts to appeal to her husband after the victory he had achieved in the Battle of Copenhagen when he was again the nation's hero. Lord Spencer had written to inform Fanny of the 'glorious victory' which put to an end activity in northern waters. Fanny wrote to congratulate her husband and thanking God for sparing his life and assuring him of her great affection for him. In July she wrote again thanking him for giving her such a generous allowance. It was the final letter written in December 1801 that was her most heartfelt appeal for his return to her. *"One thing I omitted in my letter of July which now I have to offer you is accommodation, a warm and comfortable house. Do, dear husband let us live together, I assure you I have but one wish in the world to please you. Let everything be buried in oblivion, it will pass like a dream. I can only entreat you to believe I am most sincerely and affectionately your wife, Frances. H. Nelson"* she had the letter sent via Davison, it was returned to her. 'Opened by mistake by Lord Nelson - but not read.'

CHAPTER TEN

'TOM TITT'

Both of the homes of the Nelsons were given up; Round Wood was put up for sale and the tenancy of the Dover Street house terminated. Fanny moved to 16 Somerset Street, close to Portman Square, which was not immediately ready for occupation. Some of their furniture was sold, some went to Fanny's house and some to Merton, Horatio's new home, including the contents of the wine cellar. Fanny in the meantime visited Bath and Norfolk, staying with the Walpoles at Wolverton and making a brief visit to Burnham, staying for two nights at the local inn and seeing her father-in-law and the Boltons.

On her return to London Josiah came to live with her. Their reunion was initially somewhat strained. They had not seen one another for eight years and Josiah had seldom written to his mother, most of the news about him having been conveyed via his stepfather. Fanny, who was now forty, appeared considerably older than her years. She was living in far grander surroundings than when they had lived at Burnham Rectory. She was now a woman in an important, though embarrassing, position. Josiah was rough and blunt. He had hoped to get a commission on the Thalia but had failed to do so, owing to the reputation he had earned himself in the past two years.

He had a grudge against life and especially towards Horatio, who had inspired him with his own enthusiasm to enter the Navy as a boy but for whom he now felt nothing but disdain. He was indignant at the way Nelson had behaved in Naples with Emma Hamilton and was mortified at the way he had treated his mother. He divulged much to Fanny about his times at sea and on shore, denying any admiration he was reputed to have for Emma. He had proved himself to be an excellent sailor and still loved the sea. He remained on half pay from the Navy until 1825. He decided to enter the world of commerce and joined a company in London dealing in investments, later moving onto the Paris Bourse.

The activities of Lord Nelson and the Hamiltons were frequently reported in the newspapers. Only occasionally were Lady Nelson's activities reported. Nelson had returned to London after the victory at Copenhagen. In September 1801 he had bought Merton Place in Surrey, about one hour's journey from London. It was surrounded by park land. Nelson no longer wanted a neat cottage, preferring something far grander. He insisted on everything in Merton being his own, whilst leaving the management of improvements at Merton to Emma who had found Merton. It was a home where he could offer hospitality to his family and friends – and eventually his daughter.

The birth of Emma's child was kept a closely guarded secret. Twin girls had been born in February 1801, one being immediately sent to a home for foundlings, and the other child was taken to a nurse in Marylebone, where she remained until taken to Merton a few weeks before Nelson departed to sea again. She was named Horatia Thompson. At her christening her name was entered in the church register as 'parents unknown, adopted child of Lord Nelson' . Fanny heard rumours of how happy and content Nelson was at Merton, living the life of a country squire with frequent visits to London.

The expenses of Merton were shared by Nelson and Sir William. Emma's extravagances were outrageous, but neither husband or lover put a stop to her spending. She decorated Merton in her own style, the rooms, staircases and hall were all covered with pictures and scenes of naval actions.

Emma tried her utmost to alienate all the family from Fanny, often distorting the truth in her vehement jealousy of her. Nelson's brother, the Rector, was now Dean of Canterbury, due to family influence. His wife became a close friend to Emma, and the Boltons could not afford to offend their brother by showing any friendliness towards Fanny. They all needed Nelson's influence and assistance as he was paying for the school fees of several of his nephews and nieces. Fanny was no longer to be called 'Aunt Frances'. Susannah Bolton was the last of the family to drop her friendship with Fanny. She had written to her in

May 1801 ... "You talk of making a visit to Wolverton ... If it does take place, I hope you will favour us with your company here, do not suffer us to take too much notice of you for fear it should injure us with Lord Nelson. I assure you I have pride as well as himself, in doing what is right and that surely is to be attentive to those who have been so to us and I am sure my brother would despise us if we acted contrary ... ".

Maurice, who had been the favourite relation of Fanny, had died very suddenly in April leaving a widow who was blind. Nelson gave her a pension of £200.

Edmund Nelson, "our father" alone remained loyal to Fanny. They had been together for long periods since her first coming to the Rectory at Burnham. She had nursed him through a long illness, and they had shared joys and sorrows. He greatly regretted "the breach" and would have been overjoyed if it could have been healed. He also was aware that his illustrious son had found happiness and contentment with Emma. He wanted to join Fanny in her home or for Fanny to join him in Bath but the idea was opposed so strongly by Nelson and Emma that instead he joined the Matchams, who were living in

Bath. He had only made one visit to Merton but on that occasion admitted that Nelson was truly happy.

In April 1802 he had written to Fanny to inform her that his daughter, Kitty Matcham, had given birth to a daughter. Six days later he was gravely ill and it was Fanny who reached his bedside before he died. That friendship was something that Emma did not destroy. Neither Lord or Lady Nelson attended the funeral, which took place at Burnham; the rest of his family were present and many friends and parishioners. Susannah Bolton wrote to Fanny to express her appreciation of her going to Bath to be at the bedside of their father. The letter ended

"I am going to Merton in about a fortnight, but dear Lady N. we cannot meet, as I wished for every body is known who visits you. Indeed I do not think I shall be permitted to go to town. But be assured I always have and shall always be your sincere friend. S. Bolton. To Viscountess Nelson, Somerset Street, Portman Square, London."

Officially Fanny was still recognised and treated as Lord Nelson's wife and as such was invited to official and Court functions, in particular the Queen's birthday reception. For fear of meeting his wife face to face Nelson avoided this function in 1801 and again in 1802. These absences were also protests by him against the fact that Lady Hamilton was never invited to Court.

Many of Nelson's friends remained friendly with Fanny: the Berrys, the Walpoles, and Captain Hardy, who regarded her as one of the best women in the world. Alexander Davidson still hoped the Nelsons might be reunited. Despite this support she was given, she felt ridiculous. She had to make a conscious effort to summon up her mental and physical resources. The 'Trio

Juncta in Uno' had become a joke. James Gillray, the cartoonist, delighted in caricaturing Emma in the newspapers. Emma's gross extravagance and her neglect of Sir William in favour of Horatio led the former to take furnished rooms in London. The trio went on a long and protracted tour of the West Country and Wales during the summer of 1802, with Lord Nelson receiving honours and acclaim all along their route and all the details appearing in the press.

The tour exhausted Sir William, who was now aged 73, and after hosting a birthday party for 100 guests at Merton they took the lease of a house in London on the pretext that it was more convenient for Nelson to attend the House of Lords from there. Sir William never got over the loss of many of his treasures. He had crated them when in Naples and sent them back to England aboard the Colossus, which was wrecked off the Scilly Isles, so close to home. They could have been sold for many thousands of pounds, which would have greatly relieved his financial difficulties. His health was deteriorating and he grew frail and weak. He died in the arms of Emma and Nelson on the 6th April 1803. He left Emma an allowance of £800 annually, the remainder of his estate being left to his nephew, Sir Charles Grenville. His body was taken by hearse to lie beside that of his first adoring wife, Catherine, in Steback Church, Pembrokeshire in Wales.

The peace between France and England had lasted only a year; neither country had ratified the Treaty of Amiens. War between them was declared in June 1803. Reports were already circulating that the French were preparing to invade England. Nelson was recalled to service and had been given command of the Victory and made Commander-in-Chief in the Mediterranean. The Spanish declared war against Britain in 1804, by which time the British fleet was then occupied in chasing the French fleet, under Villeneuve, to the West

Indies and back until confrontation off Cadiz on the 21st October 1805. The Battle of Trafalgar and the part Nelson played in securing total victory over the French has been recounted by many historians over the past two centuries. Before breathing his last breath the words spoken and his thoughts were of Emma.

The news of the success at Trafalgar and the death of Nelson did not reach the Admiralty until 6 November, sixteen days after the event. It was conveyed there by two Naval officers bearing the sealed dispatches of Admiral Collingwood. There is, however, a tradition in West Cornwall that the news of Trafalgar and the hero's demise, was announced in the town of Penzance before it reached London. The schooner, the Pickle, bringing the dispatch to Falmouth on 3 November, passed the news to a Penzance fishing boat off the Lizard peninsula. They brought it ashore to Mayor Thomas Giddy who was officiating at a ball in the Assembly Rooms at the rear of the Union Hotel in Chapel Street, Penzance. Immediately he called the dancing to a halt and from the balcony announced both the triumph and the tragedy. He followed this up with the declaration of a memorial service and procession to be held each year at the Parish Church of Madron (the original mother church of Penzance), a tradition carried out to this day in the nearby village.

In London the news was issued promptly by the Admiralty to the London Gazette Extraordinary. The Controller of the Navy Board was delegated to inform Emma. On the same date as the news was received in London, the First Lord of the Admiralty, Lord Barham, sent this letter to Lady Nelson,

"Madam - It is with the utmost concern that in the midst of victory I have to inform you of the death of your illustrious partner Lord Viscount Nelson. After leading the British fleet into close action with the enemy and seeing their defeat he fell by a musket ball entering his chest. It is the death he wished for and less

to be regretted on his own account. But the public loss is irretrievable. I can only add that events of this kind do not happen by chance. I recommend your Ladyship to His protection who alone is able to save or destroy. Being with much esteem madam your faithful and most obedient servant, Barham."

The whole nation mourned for him. He had been famous in his life but he became immortal by his death, his passing outshone the victory he had won at Trafalgar. His body was brought back to Portsmouth in the Victory in early December and was then brought ashore three weeks later to Greenwich, where he lay in state. The Times newspaper, 7th January 1806, reported that,

'Thousands of people paid their tribute of melancholy respect at the temporary shrine of the departed hero ... and many more thousands were turned away unsatisfied ... many were crushed in a dreadful manner ... it was scarcely possible to check the impetuosity of the multitude. Within, however all was conducted with order ... Among the visitations of yesterday were numbers of high rank and fashion, her Grace of Devonshire and many of her noble friends were in the throng. A vast number of military officers also attended to pay their last tributes of respect to departed heroism, and to contemplate the noblest stimulus to gallant deeds'.

His funeral took place on the 9th January in St Paul's Cathedral. Thirty one admirals, one hundred captains, the Prince of Wales, Prince William and many other prominent people attended the service and burial.

Neither Lady Nelson nor Lady Hamilton attended the funeral. Fanny grieved in private, a grief that was very profound. She received numerous letters of condolence. Lady Walpole wrote a very touching letter to Josiah offering his mother comfort, knowing how much she had loved Nelson. Lady Berry offered to come to comfort and support her whenever she needed her. Her brother-in-law wrote, expressing the hope that they could renew their acquaintance with each other...'which untoward circumstances have occasioned some interruption of.' He was to inform her of the contents of the last will of the 'great man.'

It was customary for a close relative of any deceased person to remain in mourning for at least two years. It is not surprising therefore that Lady Nelson's dressmakers account in 1806 totalled £45/17s. From E. Franks (Milliner and Dressmaker to their Royal Highnesses the Princess of Wales and the Duchess of York). Fanny bought a rich black silk gown made up complete with lining, Persian sleeve lining, fine muslin weepers, (widow's white cuffs.) In May she bought a black crepe bonnet, a black twill sarsnet dress, a full twill dress gown, jet ornaments, a black crepe turban, black Spanish cloak trimmed round with black crepe, a black crepe hat and flowers and more besides. The account was sent to her at Clifton, where she was staying to avoid London.

There were legal affairs to be dealt with, mainly concerning Nelson's will. The title was inherited by Reverend William Nelson, who also received a pension of £5,000 a year and a vast sum of money to purchase a Nelson family estate. Fanny received a pension of £2,000 a year for life to add to the £1,000 she received annually from Nelson's estate. She had tried, through her lawyers, to get some further payment from the estate but the new Viscount Nelson would not agree to this. In the Will there were instructions for the executors to have sixty gold memorial rings made and distributed to close family and friends as named by him. Fanny did not receive a ring, Emma did.

Emma and Horatia, whom Nelson loved more than anyone else, were ignored by the state. They were left Merton and £2,000 by Nelson as well as £4,000 in trust for Horatia. A codicil to the will requested that Emma should be given a state pension for the role she had played in assisting Britain when she was at the Court of Naples. The contents of the codicil appeared in full in

The Times, where it was later suggested by a correspondent that Lady Hamilton should retire to her original obscurity and not intrude further upon Public Notice and should be assisted by the present Earl Nelson to do so. The publicity and the public mourning slowly faded away leaving Fanny and Emma to grieve in their separate ways.

CHAPTER ELEVEN

EXMOUTH 1807 - 1831

Lady Nelson went to live in Exmouth in 1807. Her first visit there had been twenty years earlier when the Nelsons returned to England, shortly after their marriage on Nevis. During those intervening years Exmouth had changed from being a small fishing village to being a popular "watering place" but remained small and select. It was visited not only by invalids but was considered during the summer months as an "eligible retreat for the children of idleness and gaiety". It had a warm and gentle climate and Lady Nelson preferred it to Sidmouth, which was larger and patronised by Royalty. The notable families who lived in the vicinity included the Ellenboroughs, the Giffords, the Nutwells and the Bystocks. The Rolle family had been responsible for much of the development. A theatre was built in 1808 and the Assembly Rooms in 1818. Families from the North of England and people retired from the East India Company were among the new residents.

Sea bathing had become as popular as taking the waters in Spa towns such as Bath and Cheltenham. The joy of 'the dip' and the medical benefits of sea water were much sought after. The bathers were transported into the sea in bathing machines pulled by a horse into about three feet of water. The bather then emerged and proceeded to take a dip having changed into a bathing garment in the privacy of the machine. There were dippers who helped the bathers, ensuring that they were properly immersed unless the bather was a proficient swimmer. Lady Nelson was not.

She was fortunate to find a small house, number 6 The Beacon which was much to her liking. It stood above the village with extensive views along the coast, and across the Exe estuary towards Dartmoor. Downstairs there were two large parlours on either side of a hallway; an attractive curved stairway led up to the bedrooms and the attics. The kitchens were in the semi basement and outside there were stables and sleeping quarters for the coachman. She engaged three maids. The lease on the house was 7 guineas per week, later she bought the house. There were some amiable people in the neighbourhood for her to socialise with, Lady Bryon lived at number 19 The Beacon.

Fanny was assured that the sea bathing, taking a 'dip', would benefit her health so she indulged in this at infrequent intervals. She went to the theatre to hear Edmund Kean reading poetry and, to see plays performed. She was conveyed everywhere in her sedan chair. On Sundays she attended church at Littleham, the Parish church, which contained memorials of the Drake family who had lived nearby. Church attendance in Nevis had been very lax, but when she went to live at Burnham Rectory with her father-in-law she attended church regularly, and continued to do so. His belief that God's hand was in everything that came to pass and the way he lived his life exemplified the principles of Christianity. 'Through God we shall do great things.' (Psalm 108) was what he had preached to Horatio.

The death of Lord Nelson had brought, perhaps, an unconscious relief to Fanny, who emerged from her period of mourning as a more robust character than previously. She had a role to play as the widow of the Nation's hero and she was proud of her position.

The first biography of Lord Nelson was published in 1806, written by James Harrison and assisted by Lady Hamilton. It caused Fanny much indignation. The following year when the Reverend J.S. Clarke and Dr J.M.M. Arthur were collecting material for an official biography, Fanny wrote to M. Arthur *"I think without exception Mr Harris's life of Lord Nelson is the basest production that was ever offered to the public. It is replete with untruths ... in regard to my son and myself - when I told my son what Mr H said in regard to his saving Lord Nelson's life at Tenerife, all the answer he made was 'God knows I saved Lord N's life at T. That's a pleasure no one can take from me."*

Fanny also wrote a memoranda of events which took place on the night Nelson lost his arm, giving the biographers the full account as Nelson had told her. The authors were given access to a very few of her personal letters from Horatio. When their book was published she bought only one copy. The Life of Horatio Nelson by Robert Southey was published first in 1813 by John Murray. This was the best biography written during Fanny's lifetime. Southey was the Poet Laureate and the biography was considered to be a masterpiece of English literature, although it was later agreed to contain historical errors, having not been well researched.

In addition to books written, portraits and pictures were painted, Nelson plates, mugs and glasses were manufactured and sold in large quantities, statues were erected, streets named after him and the highest monument in existence in a new London Square was being planned. The Patriotic Fund at Lloyds presented Fanny with a silver gilt vase commemorating the victory at Trafalgar; it was shaped like an urn and stood on a pedestal. It cost £650 and took four years to be made, owing to the inscriptions on one side and on the second side a picture in relief of an emblem of merit. Earl Nelson received a similar vase.

Lady Hamilton's name had slowly ceased to be an item of news or the subject of gossip. Following the death of Nelson she was reported to be prostrate with grief for two weeks. On several occasions she was seen at a dramatic presentation of The Death of Nelson with the singer Braham in the principal role. Emma added to the drama by fainting conspicuously at each performance. Her demise was a story of debt, drink and ridicule. Her debts through gambling and drink accumulated so quickly that less than three years after Trafalgar, Merton House had to be sold by her trustees. She received £3,700 and the contents of the house brought £2,500, which sum was handed to her creditors. She tried in vain to extract as much money as possible from Nelson's estate but the new Earl Nelson and Hazelwood, the lawyer, opposed every request she made. In their turn they managed to extract from her several items that had been presented to Nelson, such as the diamond Aigretter, the sword presented to him by the King of Naples and other gifts.

She had to sell her London home and moved to Richmond. A few of Nelson's friends sent her small amounts of money. The Matchams sent her £100. Her appeal to her old friend Queen Carolina as well as to Prince William were both to no avail. When she was sued for debt by a coach builder she was sent to a debtors prison. On release she sold all her remaining effects and with £50 she set sail for France with Horatia, arriving at Calais in July 1814.

Emma lived in a farmhouse near the town, taking Horatia to school every day, drinking too much porter and always being short of money. Six months later she died, a simple funeral being arranged by a moneylender in Calais. The service was attended by English Naval Officers stationed at Calais, who followed the coffin to the grave. Emma never told Horatia that she was her real mother nor that Nelson was her real father rather than her adoptive father. Horatia was rescued from France by the Matchams and lived with them in Norfolk until she married the Reverend William Ward in 1822. Fanny learnt about Emma's death but knew little about the other events in her life.

Emma's face had been her fortune. She had been a great lover - Featherstonhaugh (the father of her first child), Grenville and Hamilton never

81

ceased to like her. She possessed charm and she played a role in the affairs of the Kingdom of the two Sicilies far above her qualifications. Her fame has remained and been the subject of biographies and novels. To Nelson she was the most precious person he had ever known.

During the winter of 1809-1810 Fanny was staying in Bath as were the Earl and Countess Nelson with their daughter, Lady Caroline Nelson. This family remained hostile to Fanny and although they were reputed to be on friendly terms with Emma had done nothing to assist her financially. Because both parties were in Bath together Lady Caroline took her parents to the house Fanny was renting. They were received by Fanny and hands were shaken but little cordiality was shown. There was no further communication between them.

Fanny was far more interested in Mrs Walter Nisbet, who was also in Bath, her husband had died on Nevis in 1798. She had returned to England with her family, her two sons entering the Indian Civil Service. Thus ended the Nisbet connection with Nevis. Much had changed there in recent years. Sugar production was on a decline, countries such as India and Brazil sold their sugar at a lower cost. It was the Act to abolish slave trading that forced many families known to Fanny to leave the Island. The movement towards the Emancipation of slavery was gaining widespread support. (Nelson had voiced his opinion in the House of Lords against the 'damnable doctrine of Wilberforce, and his hypocritical allies'.) Fanny also kept in touch with Anne Nisbet, her spinster sister-in-law, sending her £30 each year and remained on close terms with the other sister-in-law, Mrs Lockhart.

The war against France had ended in 1814, following the Battle of Waterloo. Napoleon had been exiled to Elba and stability in Europe seemed likely. The British looked across the channel for trade, for business, for travel.

82

Josiah was already established in business, marketing foreign investments in the City of London. He had been lent £1,000 by his mother to establish himself and was making a success in his career. He lived in the house Fanny had bought in London, 23 Harley Street, and visited her in Exmouth during the summer. He was interested in the harbour having never lost his love of the sea nor his ability as a sailor. He had a sailing boat built for himself, large and strong enough for cross channel sailing and to accommodate a crew of three.

By 1819 Josiah had extended his business interests to Paris, marketing investments and dealing in French Rentes, stocks and shares and consuls. His mother had a young lady companion living with her in Exmouth, Frances Herbert Evans, she and her family having moved there from Wales. Josiah, who until now had resisted marriage, fell in love with Frances and their marriage took place at Littleham Church, the marriage certificate being signed by Lady Nelson.

Fanny was delighted that Josiah had found such a suitable and amiable wife and the two women had a great affection for each other. The Nisbets made frequent trips to France in the newly built boat until they bought a house in Paris in 1822. Fanny continued to enjoy living in Exmouth for most of the year. The local newspaper reported details of a dinner and ball given by the Dowager Duchess of Bronte in the London hotel Exmouth, listing the notable people who had attended. That was the year of King George IV's Coronation. Travel had become easier due to improvements in the roads and better designs of private carriages, it was less of a hardship to travel between Bath, London and Exmouth.

There is an account of 'Viscountess Nelson' attending a ball at Broadstairs in November, 1809 in the journal of Lady Nugent (edited 1839). She was reported as being shocked at Lady Campbell and the Duchess of Manchester who each asked their own partners to dance. Fanny assured her hostess, Lady Nugent, that Lady Campbell must be mad or perhaps even worse for the latter wore half-boots and had a dog called the Devil. Fanny expected people of high rank to show dignity and refinement; immoderation did not please her.

In 1823 Fanny made her first journey to France. This involved a coach from London to Dover, crossing the Channel, staying in Calais before taking a further coaches to Paris. Since parts of the city had been demolished by the populace during the revolution much of it was being newly built, streets avenues, squares, bridges and parks. The Arc D'Etoile was not yet completed, the roads and pathways often deep in mud and gutters ran down the middle of the streets. There were only a few houses in the Champs Elysee where Josiah lived. English people were flocking to Paris, society, men of fashion and distinction. There was a popular song, "All the world's in Paris". Fanny met people of high rank whilst she was there and received invitations to the British Embassy where receptions, dejeuners and balls were given on a magnificent scale. She met the Duchess of Wellington whilst there and was known as 'the little Viscountess'. It was a great joy for her to see Josiah so successful in his work and so happy with his growing family. Their first child had died before his first birthday but more had been born since then. The family travelled to Lake Geneva and met Lord Byron there who took them in his rowing boat on the lake. To the utter dismay of Fanny, one of the children fell into the water but was instantly rescued by Byron. She toured through other parts of France, to Lyons and Colmar seeing friends in each place. She still had a good command of the French language. Often she was left in charge of the grandchildren whilst their parents travelled around France and Spain attending to their business affairs. She was reputed to be the kindest and most sympathetic of Grandmothers During her first visit to Paris the Matcham family was also there. Their daughter Harriet called on Fanny and was warmly received. Friendly relations were restored between Fanny and the Matchams, who visited her often. Mrs Matcham (Kitty) and Mrs Frances Nelson were on most affectionate terms and all the past divisions were forgotten. Having adopted Horatia Nelson the Matchams had undoubtly learnt much about Lady Hamilton and changed their attitude towards their sister-in -law.

The house in Exmouth was considered too big now that the Nisbet family was resident in Paris. In 1829 Fanny bought a smaller house in Louisa Terrace, which was close to the Beacon. Early the following year she met King William during a visit to Brighton. He had just succeeded his brother George IV to the throne. He had always remained a friend to Nelson (and had flirted with Emma much to Horatio's consternation). Now the widow and the monarch recalled the party on Nevis when they had danced together and the wedding which had taken place there. Did King William recall what he had predicted about the marriage, that Nelson had needed a nurse not a wife? Fanny had been the former and Emma the latter.

The artist Sir William Beechey painted a portrait of Lady Nelson during that year. In it she is wearing an elaborate dress and a large bonnet, and is looking her age, which was then 69. The artist has portrayed her with the hint of a smile on her lips, giving the impression of a stately and dignified character. Had the portrait been painted a year later the expression on the her face would have been very different, for Josiah had died on the 14th July 1830. The cause of his death was oedema, referred to as dropsy.

Josiah's body, together with the remains of three of his children who had died previously and had been buried in a Parisian cemetery, were brought back to Exmouth for burial on English soil. This operation was carried out under most difficult circumstances as Paris was for three days in the midst of an attempted coup d'etat. The revolutionaries forced their way into the convent where the bodies were lying prior to shipment across the channel, but fortunately the bodies and the nuns were left unmolested.

Mrs Nisbet and her family had a dramatic escape from Paris. They were obliged to dress up to resemble French peasants and to make their way through northern France before crossing the channel, arriving on British soil and making their way to Fanny's London home. The coffins were brought across the channel in a French schooner and then by pilot boat into Exmouth harbour. The funeral service took place at Littleham and they were buried in the churchyard. Josiah's widow, his mother and his three remaining daughters shared one another's grief. Josiah left a considerable fortune in Paris which was given to his wife in trust for his daughters 'on condition they were brought up to attend the Anglican Church and to live in England during their minorities.'

Fanny never recovered from the fact that Josiah had pre-deceased her. She found little incentive to go on living. She now spent most of her final days in her home in London, sharing it with a distant cousin by marriage, Lady Franklin. She had suffered from a chronic bronchial condition which subsequently developed into pneumonia. During the last weeks of her life she had been in considerable pain and had been nursed by her cousin. She died on the 4th May 1831.

In her will she left her money £4,000 to her daughter-in-law and then to her eldest grandchild Frances Herbert Nelson.

"The remains of the late Viscountess Nelson were, on Monday last removed from her residence in Upper Harley Street, for internment in the family vault at Littleham, near Exmouth, followed by Lord Bridport, General Egerton and

other relations and friends of the deceased and a long line of carriages including those of Lord Nelson and Vernon, and Sir Thomas Hardy" Extract from The Times, 13th May 1831.

POSTSCRIPT

LADY NELSON and Nevis

A plaque commemorating the marriage of Horatio to Frances hangs on the old gatepost of Montpelier House. There is a Nelson Museum in Charlestown. The island has been independent since 1982. It is now a favoured holiday island with several high class hotels and many holiday homes built by Americans and Europeans.

A Lady Nelson Memorial Fund with a target of £4,000 to restore and repair the tomb at Littleham was met and restoration has taken place.

Frances Nisbet died in Cheltenham in 1864. Her daughter Frances died in 1894, Mary died in 1915 and Georgina died in 1904. They had all married and had offspring.

THE NELSON FAMILY

The Reverend William, Earl Nelson died in 1835, his son Horatio had died of typhoid in 1808 and the earldom was then inherited by Susannah Bolton's son Tom in 1835.

Susannah died in 1813 predeceasing her husband. Catherine Nelson (Kitty) died in 1842.

Using the money bequeathed by the Nation at Nelson's death, a house was bought near Salisbury and renamed Trafalgar House, it cost £99,000. It was passed down through the family until the fourth Earl Nelson died, unmarried, in 1947. It had changed hands several times and in 1992 was for sale, price guide £1.5 million.

The Viscountcy is still in existence.

LADY HAMILTON

In Calais a monument to her was erected in 1993.

Source material

The letters used in this book have been taken from Nelson's Letters to His Wife edited by G.P.B. Naish, published by Routledge & Paul, 1858.

Three volumes of letters from Nelson written during 15 years of their marriage are preserved in the Nelson Museum at Monmouth, some of which have been seen by the author of this monograph. Other letters are in the National Maritime Museum at Greenwich.

Sixty-four letters from Lady Nelson to her husband, written between 1794 and 1797-1800 are in the British Library [MSS 34988 and MSS 34902-34992].

The National Maritime Museum paid £138,650 for 72 unpublished letters from Nelson's wife, Frances, to Davison. The letters reveal that she went to great lengths to win Nelson back from Lady Hamilton, his mistress.

The Times, 7 January 1806, and 13 May 1831.

Bibliography

Cundall, Frank (Editor, 1939) Lady Nugent's Journal

D'Auvergne, Edmund B (1936) The Dear Emma, London: Harrap

Edgington, Harry (1981) Nelson, The Hero and the Lover, London: Hamlyn Paperback

Gerin, Winifred (1970) Horatia Nelson, Oxford: OUP

Hibbert, Christopher (1991) Captain Gronow

Keate, E M (1939) Nelson's Wife, London: Cassell

Nelson Society & the 1805 Club, Journals

Pares, Richard (1950) The West Indian Fortune, London: Longmans

Pocock, Tom (1987) Horatio Nelson, London: Bodley Head

        (1999) Nelson's Women, London: Andre Deutsch

Russell, Jack (1969) Nelson and the Hamiltons, London: Anthony Bond

Stokes, H G (1947) The English Seaside, Sylvan Press

Southey, Robert (1906 edition of 1813 original) The Life of Horatio Nelson, London: J M Dent (1906)

Sweete, Rev. John. Devon's age of Elegance, edited by Peter Hunt. Devon Books 1984